**New Directions for
Institutional Research**

Robert K. Toutkoushian
EDITOR-IN-CHIEF

J. Fredericks Volkwein
Paul D. Umbach
ASSOCIATE EDITORS

Assessing Student Outcomes: Why, Who, What, How?

J. Fredericks Volkwein

EDITOR

Assessment Supplement 2009
Jossey-Bass
San Francisco

Assessing Student Outcomes: Why, Who, What, How?
J. Fredericks Volkwein (ed.)
New Directions for Institutional Research, Assessment Supplement 2009
Robert K. Toutkoushian, Editor-in-Chief

New Directions for Institutional Research (ISSN 0271-0579, electronic ISSN 1536-075X) is part of The Jossey-Bass Higher and Adult Education Series and is published quarterly by Wiley Subscription Services, Inc., A Wiley Company, at Jossey-Bass, 989 Market Street, San Francisco, California 94103-1741 (publication number USPS 098-830). Periodicals Postage Paid at San Francisco, California, and at additional mailing offices. POSTMASTER: Send address changes to New Directions for Institutional Research, Jossey-Bass, 989 Market Street, San Francisco, California 94103-1741.

Subscriptions cost $109 for individuals and $264 for institutions, agencies, and libraries in the United States. See order form at end of book.

Editorial correspondence should be sent to Robert K. Toutkoushian, Educational Leadership and Policy Studies, Education 4220, 201 N. Rose Ave., Indiana University, Bloomington, IN 47405.

New Directions for Institutional Research is indexed in *CIJE: Current Index to Journals in Education* (ERIC), *Contents Pages in Education* (T&F), and *Current Abstracts* (EBSCO).

Microfilm copies of issues and chapters are available in 16mm and 35mm, as well as microfiche in 105mm, through University Microfilms, Inc., 300 North Zeeb Road, Ann Arbor, Michigan 48106-1346.

www.josseybass.com

THE ASSOCIATION FOR INSTITUTIONAL RESEARCH was created in 1966 to benefit, assist, and advance research leading to improved understanding, planning, and operation of institutions of higher education. Publication policy is set by its Publications Committee.

For information about the Association for Institutional Research, write to the following address:

AIR Executive Office
1435 E. Piedmont Drive
Suite 211
Tallahassee, FL 32308-7955

(850) 385-4155

air@mailer.fsu.edu
http://airweb.org

CONTENTS

EDITOR'S NOTES

This is the latest volume in the New Directions for Institutional Research (NDIR) Assessment Series. In order to accommodate the new series and with the encouragement of the Association for Institutional Research, NDIR has expanded from four volumes per year to five. Each year these volumes address and illuminate a particular aspect within the complicated topic of assessment. The Assessment Supplement is designed for higher education professionals who seek a fuller understanding of student outcomes assessment and its role in institutional effectiveness.

The volume summarizes the best of what we know about assessing student outcomes. Each chapter provides a foundation for examining the why, who, what, and how of assessment. Few other topics are more important and complicated than outcomes assessment. The needs of students and the areas of their learning vary highly among institutions and degree programs. Students are diverse, and the dimensions of the learning processes in American higher education are extremely complex. Thus, assessing student performance is complex and, hence, difficult to summarize.

This volume has direct linkages to several courses in Penn State's online Institutional Research Certificate program. The volume as a whole is designed to support the lessons in *Assessing Student Outcomes and Evaluating Academic Programs*. Chapters One through Four draw on some of the assessment and evaluation readings and materials covered in selected units of *IR Foundations and Fundamentals*. This volume also discusses relevant literature and theories of student outcomes that are contained in *Studying Students and Student Affairs*, as well as in the *Assessment* and *Foundations* courses. Persistence models and retention theories identified in these courses and this NDIR volume are relevant also to *Conducting Enrollment Management Studies*. Finally, Penn State's course in *Research Design,* with its emphasis on measurement issues and survey research, provides an analytical foundation for any assessment activity. Thus, readers will find that this NDIR volume provides the intellectual foundation and supporting resources for an array of domains that are central to professional institutional research practice in higher education.

We need to place the assessment journey within a context and within the environment that is heavily shaping what we do. Thus, Chapter One examines why assessment is so important. The internal need for improvement is even greater than the external demands for accountability, accreditation, and performance reporting, but together they provide both inspirational and pragmatic foundations for assessing student outcomes. In Chapter Two, I propose a model for assessing institutional effectiveness. The

NEW DIRECTIONS FOR INSTITUTIONAL RESEARCH, Assessment Supplement 2009, Spring 2010 © Wiley Periodicals, Inc.
Published online in Wiley InterScience (www.interscience.wiley.com) • DOI: 10.1002/ir.326

five parts of the model summarize the steps for evaluating institutions, programs, faculty, and students. In recent years, evidence of student outcomes has become one of the key indicators of institutional effectiveness, especially as it is viewed by accrediting associations, as well as by many boards of trustees and state higher education governing boards.

Chapters Three and Four discuss some common campus obstacles to assessment implementation and suggest ways to overcome them. Chapter Three is a reprint of Patrick Terenzini's "Assessment with Open Eyes," a landmark discussion of the pitfalls of assessing student outcomes, published in 1989 in the *Journal of Higher Education*. In my opinion, it is the most valuable 20 pages ever written on this topic. In Chapter Four, I extend this discussion with some practical suggestions derived from assessment experiences at a research university.

The remaining chapters dive more completely into assessment by examining the what and how of this topic, including several outcomes assessment models. Chapters Five through Eight examine the core academic outcomes: basic skills, general education, attainment in the major, and personal growth. In Chapter Nine, we examine alumni studies, regarded by many as the most cost-effective way to collect useful assessment information.

Chapter Ten takes a page from Penn State's research design course and discusses several data and measurement issues: the uses of standardized testing versus self-reported measures, attributing causality and estimating unique effects, dealing with missing data, and weighting data. Chapter Eleven concludes the volume by summarizing some effective dissemination and reporting strategies once assessment findings are in hand. This chapter reviews some best practices for reporting research results to diverse audiences and addresses written, visual, and verbal presentations.

Each chapter in this volume lists supplementary reading and Web links that provide additional information to explore each topic in greater depth. I am grateful to my graduate students for their many contributions to this volume and to my thinking about outcomes assessment over the years.

J. Fredericks Volkwein
Editor

J. FREDERICKS VOLKWEIN is emeritus professor of higher education at The Pennsylvania State University and a former director of the Center for the Study of Higher Education.

1

This chapter discusses the drivers for assessment and enables readers to understand the tensions arising within colleges and universities in regard to accountability, accreditation, and performance evaluation.

The Assessment Context: Accreditation, Accountability, and Performance

J. Fredericks Volkwein

A diverse society has created a diverse education system, which in turn requires diverse and complex mechanisms of quality control. The diversity and complexity of our industrial, service, and knowledge-based economy, with its vast variety of occupations and dynamic labor markets, heavily influences the curricular structures and academic profiles of American colleges and universities. To be successful, institutions of higher education must meet the educational needs of individuals with different economic statuses, ages, occupational goals, educational aspirations, educational preparation, and family circumstances. These same forces—employers and students—drive curricular diversity as colleges and universities attempt to serve the needs of their local, regional, or national communities, along with the needs of students through an array of academic programs and courses. This open and competitive system has generated institutions of higher education that vary significantly in terms of mission, sources of funding, size, student body characteristics, curricular offerings, administrative complexity, and resources.

While the "ratings game" encourages institutions to become more alike, local control is a strong American value that encourages the opposite. Moreover, the openness and competitiveness of the system encourages new educational providers. Driven by a diverse economy and society, higher education is now a complex industry of public and private educational

New Directions for Institutional Research, Assessment Supplement 2009, Spring 2010 © Wiley Periodicals, Inc.
Published online in Wiley InterScience (www.interscience.wiley.com) • DOI: 10.1002/ir.327

providers, and an array of quality assurance, accreditation, and certification mechanisms has evolved reflecting this complexity.

Assessing for Internal Improvement Versus Evaluating for External Accountability

Many offices of institutional research now divide their time almost equally between the external and the internal organizational roles. The internal role includes providing data and analysis and survey research to assist managerial policymaking, enrollment management, and student outcomes assessment, among others. The externally focused responsibilities include forecasting admissions applications, benchmarking the institution against national and peer databases, transmitting official numbers to government agencies and guidebooks, and occasionally giving research papers and workshops at conferences.

The classic Janusian challenge for most institutional researchers is to resolve the potential conflict between these internal and the external roles. In public and private institutions alike, they face the need to improve themselves and become better teachers, learners, scholar-researchers, and administrators. To accomplish this, they need to expose their weaknesses and identify what needs to be changed. However, the very act of such openness runs the danger of reducing the institution's enrollment appeal and threatening its revenues, especially in an atmosphere of fierce competition and performance funding. As one writer puts it, "The spirit of assessment requires a diligent search for bad news, but accountability encourages the opposite" (Peters, 1994, p. 23).

The Inspirational and the Pragmatic. To resolve this tension, I like to think about these opposite forces as the inspirational versus the pragmatic: doing something because you want to versus doing something because you have to.

The inspirational foundation for evaluation and assessment is doing it for self-improvement, especially for the enhancement of student learning and growth. We in higher education are at our best when we carry out educational change, assessment, and evaluation not to please external stakeholders but to satisfy ourselves—to achieve an organizational climate of ongoing development and continuing improvement.

The pragmatic foundation for evaluation and assessment recognizes the external need to demonstrate accountability to stakeholders: legislators and trustees, taxpayers and tuition payers. Moreover, assessing institutional effectiveness enables universities to successfully compete for enrollments and resources and gain a strategic advantage over others. In an atmosphere of scarcity, campuses that can measure their effectiveness and reshape themselves will do better in the competition for enrollments, resources, and faculty than campuses that cannot do so. And on each campus, the academic departments and programs that are able to provide presidents and provosts with evidence about the impacts they are having on their students will be more successful in the competition for campus resources than academic units not able to provide such evidence.

Thus, the simultaneous and competing needs for both internal improvement and external accountability provide the first foundation for demonstrating institutional and program effectiveness and guiding the institutional research assessment agenda. The regional accrediting associations also are helping to resolve this dichotomy by requiring each campus to present evidence of student learning and growth as a key component in demonstrating the institution's effectiveness. Over the past decade, this pressure has been especially visible in the publications and written standards of the Middle States Commission on Higher Education, North Central Association of Colleges and Schools, and the Western Association of Schools and Colleges. To be accredited, each institution is expected to gather and present evidence that it is accomplishing its educational goals and producing improvements both inside and outside the classroom: improvements in the experience of new students, academic advisement, mentoring, residential life, teaching effectiveness, and the general education curriculum. The other regional accreditation bodies and several of the discipline-based accreditors (especially the Accreditation Board for Engineering and Technology and the Association to Advance Collegiate Schools of Business) have strengthened their demands for outcomes evidence as well. Consequently, the accrediting bodies properly call attention to the twin purposes of assessment: internal improvement and external accountability.

Accreditation Diversity and Complexity. Accreditation and quality assurance activity focuses on three major levels: institutional, programmatic, and individual. True, at most universities, it seems as if there is an unending stream of self-study documents and site visit teams from regional, state, and discipline-based bodies. But at least these accreditation groups focus on educational effectiveness rather than on the latest guidebook ratings.

At the institutional or campus level, the U.S. Department of Education and the Council for Higher Education Accreditation recognize six voluntary associations that accredit nationally and six that accredit regionally. Five of the six that accredit nationally limit their scope to distance education providers, rabbinical schools, and Christian and other theological colleges and schools. The sixth agency that accredits nationally is the Accrediting Council of Independent College and Schools, which accredits over six hundred independent, nonprofit career schools, and colleges operating in the United States and abroad.

The oldest and best-known vehicles for providing external accountability and quality assurance are the processes designed collaboratively by the member institutions of the six regions: Middle States, New England, North Central, Northwest, Southern, and Western. Each has developed (and frequently enhances) elaborate processes for the conduct of institutional self-study, review, and reaccreditation. Regional accreditation is a process based on self-review and peer assessment. It is comprehensive in scope, covering an institution's financial status, governance, faculty and staff relations, institutional achievements, student services, and student learning outcomes. Reviews typically are conducted on a ten-year cycle (shorter cycles are used in the case of serious problems within an institution).

At the program level, the picture is more complicated. Specialized academic and vocational accrediting bodies and professional societies scrutinize and accredit officially recognized programs in an array of specialties. This quality assurance activity began in some of the oldest disciplines, like medicine, law, business, and theology, and now includes nearly one hundred fields of study, ranging from business to music, chemistry to journalism, librarianship to nursing, forestry to physical therapy, and public administration to teacher education. Institutions are eager to meet the standards set by these professional organizations because accredited programs attract the best students, as well as federal and state funding.

Even in the absence of external accreditors, most campuses have their own faculty-led program review processes. Campus strategic plans almost everywhere now depend on realistic assessments of internal strengths and weaknesses matched against external constraints and opportunity. Thus, nearly every institution has developed its own program review and quality control measures, often coordinating these internal reviews with those of the specialized discipline or profession.

In addition, in many parts of the nation, there are state-mandated periodic reviews of academic programs, especially at the graduate level. Sometimes these are coordinated with and draw on, rather than override, the internal and external academic program review processes.

Finally, at the individual level, there is an array of mechanisms for credentialing, licensing, and certifying professional and vocational practitioners in fields such as accounting, law, medicine, engineering, architecture, dentistry, nursing, pharmacy, social work, and teaching. Some of these take the form of national or state examinations, internships or clinical experiences, or a combination of these. Prominent examples include the bar exam for lawyers, the CPA exam for accountants, the Fundamentals of Engineering and Professional Engineering exams for engineers, the PRAXIS for teachers, and the medical boards and other specialty exams for physicians, dentists, nurses, psychologists, pharmacists, and other health care professionals.

Accreditation Review Process. As the number and level of requirements for each profession grows, the control of knowledge by specialized accrediting bodies increases, as does the importance of the accreditation review. In general, the procedures for institutional and program-level accreditation, although conducted by different accrediting associations, have many similar features. The institutional reaccreditation process typically has three components:

NEW DIRECTIONS FOR INSTITUTIONAL RESEARCH • DOI: 10.1002/ir

1. A self-study is prepared by the college or university to be reviewed that responds to the evaluation criteria established by the accreditation body.
2. A team of peer evaluators from other higher education institutions visit the institution and gather additional evidence, which they then submit in a report.
3. Based on the self-study, the site visit report, and the institution's response, the accreditation body decides to accredit, accredit with conditions, or not to accredit the institution or program under review.

Institutional reaccreditation often begins years before the review, with negotiations over the nature of the review, the focus of the self-study, the collection of evidence, and the composition of the visiting team. Perhaps the most elaborate of the regional review processes is the one in the Western Association of Schools and Colleges region. This is a long, two-stage review cycle that first judges institutional capacity and then institutional effectiveness. After the four-year process is completed, the institution, if all goes well, starts preparing for the next review cycle about six years after the commission action (sooner if all does not go well).

The old accreditation philosophy, most dominant before the 1980s, encouraged institutions to maximize the quality of the inputs in order to guarantee the quality of the outputs. While the accreditation pressure for maximizing input quality has diminished, growing external attention to performance outputs and outcomes (like academic achievement and graduation rates and faculty publications) has forced us as researchers to start at the end and look backward at the conditions that produce favorable performance. The empirical connections between high inputs and high outputs remain strong. Institutions everywhere are finding that it is in their self-interest to devote continuing attention to the quality of their faculty and student credentials on entry. Studies (Volkwein and Sweitzer, 2006; Sweitzer and Volkwein, 2009) confirm that institutional reputation and prestige are highly predictable from admissions selectivity indicators, enrollment size, and resources.

The new accreditation philosophy, growing in strength since 1990, encourages institutions and their stakeholders to measure the outcomes, that is, to judge the results of educational programs. While most of us are more comfortable with this approach, it runs the danger of providing information too late in the process to render anything but a summative acceptable-versus-unacceptable judgment. Thus, too much of a focus on outcomes may not provide the information needed for internal development and educational enhancement.

Therefore, there is now a renewed interest in process measures on the theory that good outcomes will not result from flawed educational processes. Measurement at critical process points enables institutions to determine which student experiences are having the greatest and least impact and to make corrective interventions as needed. Moreover, the

NEW DIRECTIONS FOR INSTITUTIONAL RESEARCH • DOI: 10.1002/ir

research evidence indicates that outcomes such as student growth and satisfaction are most heavily influenced by campus experiences that produce student academic and social integration, which in turn produce favorable student outcomes.

Thus, we have for institutional researchers the ideal jobs bill:

- The need to measure and improve inputs because of their strong empirical connection to important outcomes like academic achievement and graduation rates
- The need to measure critical processes because of their role in student integration and growth and because such measurement facilitates corrective intervention
- The need to measure a variety of outputs and outcomes because results matter the most

In short, we need to measure everything.

Summary of Accreditation Trends. The accreditation process has undergone dramatic changes in the past twenty years (Ewell, 2005; Wolff, 2005), and these changes have a direct impact on the nature of institutional research, especially at the campus level. One clear trend places student outcomes assessment at the center of the accreditation review. Accreditation bodies, not only at the regional level but also in many disciplines (like engineering and business), have shifted their policies and processes away from meeting rigid quantitative standards for inputs and resources and toward judging educational effectiveness from measurable outcomes. This paradigm shift was led by several of the regional accreditors (most prominently Middle States, North Central, and Western), which revised their manuals and review processes to give greater attention to student learning outcomes and program goal attainment as the institution's demonstration of its educational effectiveness. These trends began in the 1980s and gathered strength during the 1990s as one accrediting group after another shifted away from bureaucratic checklist approaches that emphasized admissions selectivity, resources, curricular requirements, facilities, faculty credentials, and seat time, now focusing their reviews instead on attaining educational objectives, particularly those related to student learning. This trend has become so widespread that several national organizations like the American Association of Colleges and Universities are bringing accrediting bodies and educational institutions together for the purpose of strengthening their shared responsibilities for student learning. Indeed, the Council of Regional Accrediting Commissions has developed principles of good practice for accrediting bodies and their member institutions to strengthen the evidence of student learning contained in the accreditation reports across the country (Wergin, 2005a, 2005b). Regional and specialized accreditors alike are investing heavily in evaluator training to ensure that each review is less personality driven and more evidence based.

A second related trend in accreditation is the greater emphasis on improvement. Outcomes assessment evidence is now the centerpiece of educational effectiveness, and using that evidence to improve is a hallmark of healthy institutions and programs. Regional and program accreditors alike are prodding all in higher education to build cultures of evidence that feed into continuous improvement systems. This trend is spreading and promises to foster self-renewing organizations. Perhaps the most dramatic initiative along these lines is North Central's Academic Quality Improvement Program (AQIP). AQIP integrates continuous improvement into a sequence of events that align with ongoing activities. The process aims to answer two overarching AQIP criteria:

- Are you doing the right things—the things that are most important in order to achieve your institution's goals?
- Are you doing things right—effectively, efficiently, in ways that truly satisfy the needs of those you serve?

A third national trend is using accreditation reviews as catalysts for institutional transformation. Embedding the accreditation review and its products in ongoing institutional processes is now quite widespread as a regional practice. In order to make the review more cost-effective, as well as to increase the benefits associated with these costly reviews, campuses and accrediting bodies alike have begun to base their accreditation self-studies and reviews on existing processes (like strategic planning or program evaluation or student services or enrollment management) rather than to generate a one-time, stand-alone self-study document that evaporates as soon as the site visit team leaves the campus. Most of the six regional accrediting bodies encourage institutions to elect this review option. Progressive campus leaders increasingly are seizing the regional reaccreditation process as a "chariot for change" (Martin, Manning, and Ramaley, 2001). Rather than viewing the accrediting process as a burden or hurdle to be overcome, presidents, provosts, and deans are viewing the self-study and team visit as an opportunity to stimulate constructive change.

A fourth trend, also aimed at reducing the cost of these multiple accreditation processes, is the combined or multiple-visit model. This occurs when several accrediting bodies agree to hold their campus site visits at the same time and the respective self-studies are coordinated, if not combined. Several universities like Binghamton University and Drexel have experimented with this arrangement. The evaluations suggest that campuses prefer combined visits because the combined self-studies and visits are less costly, but that the specialized accreditation groups (like engineering and business) view them as less effective than separated reviews.

Measuring Educational Effectiveness

In higher education, we think we know how to measure efficiency and cost, but we do not agree about what it is that constitutes educational effectiveness. There are at least three competing models or philosophies about what constitutes excellence in higher education (Burke and Serban, 1998; Burke and Minassians, 2002; Volkwein, 2007).

First, the academic community traditionally embraces the resource/reputation model, disapprovingly articulated by Astin (1985). This model assumes that an institution's quality is indicated by its reputation ratings, financial resources, faculty credentials, student test scores, external funding, and rankings by experts. Under this model, faculty, sometimes joined by accreditation bodies, argue for more resources to support educational effectiveness and to boost the institution's academic standing. This drives up costs and attends to inputs rather than outcomes.

Second, many parents, students, and student affairs professionals cling to a client-centered model. Derived from the literature on quality management, this market-oriented, customer-centered model emphasizes all possible student services, faculty availability and attentiveness, student and alumni satisfaction and feedback, and low tuition and high aid. Seymour (1992) articulates this model in his book *On Q: Causing Quality in Higher Education*. Under this model, the first priority of a college or university is to fulfill the needs of students, parents, employers, and other "customers" of higher education. Institutions that best meet the needs of their constituents are considered to be the most effective. Therefore, an organization's customers, rather than the views of experts, define quality. Good customer service is very labor intensive and emphasizes student experiences over student outcomes.

Third, the civic and government community generally believes in the strategic investment model (Burke and Minassians, 2002; Volkwein, 2007). This model emphasizes the importance of return on investment, cost-benefit, and results-oriented and productivity measures such as admissions yield, graduation rates, time to degree, and expenditures per student. Under this model, government officials and even trustees evaluate each new initiative in light of its perceived payoff. This is the only one of the three dominant models that has the potential to dampen costs.

In any case, these competing views of educational excellence are interpreted differently by different higher education stakeholders. Hence, there is a potential for misunderstanding, if not outright conflict, and presidents frequently feel caught in the middle between faculty and accreditors, students and parents, government officials and trustees. Frequently institutional researchers are asked by their presidents to help develop multiple responses to multiple audiences.

Hence, efficiency joins accountability and effectiveness as a third major public concern. The costs of higher education constitute an enormous national investment. No longer is it sufficient to demonstrate student success alone. Colleges and universities must also demonstrate that teaching, research, and service programs are being conducted economically. Such concerns stimulate current legislative and trustee interest in class size, faculty workload, administrative salaries, time to degree, loan default, economic impact, and research productivity, among others.

The Connection Between Student Outcomes Assessment and Institutional Effectiveness

Chapter Two places the topic of outcomes assessment within the larger topic of institutional effectiveness. Student learning outcomes are central to the purpose of educational organizations. The greater the evidence of congruence between organizational outcomes and the statements of mission, goals, and objectives, the more institutional effectiveness is demonstrated, and the more likely is reaccreditation. The accreditation process, then, may be thought of as an attempt to examine the connection between desired and actual outcomes, with the assessment process providing much of the evidence. Although institutional effectiveness may be demonstrated in a variety of ways, student outcomes assessment supplies some of the most important documentation for institutions with educational missions. Student outcomes assessment is the act of assembling and analyzing both qualitative and quantitative teaching and learning outcomes evidence in order to examine their congruence with an institution's stated purposes and educational objectives.

References

Astin, A. *Achieving Educational Excellence: A Critical Assessment of Priorities and Practices in Higher Education*. San Francisco: Jossey-Bass, 1985.

Burke, J. C., and Minassians, H. P. (eds.). *Reporting Higher Education Results: Missing Links in the Performance Chain*. New Directions for Institutional Research, no. 116. San Francisco: Jossey-Bass, 2002.

Burke, J. C., and Serban, A.M. (eds.). *Performance Funding for Public Higher Education: Fad or Trend?* New Directions for Institutional Research, no. 97. San Francisco: Jossey-Bass, 1998.

Ewell, P. T. "Can Assessment Serve Accountability? It Depends on the Question." In J. C. Burke (ed.), *Achieving Accountability in Higher Education*. San Francisco: Jossey-Bass, 2005.

Martin, R. R., Manning, K., and Ramaley, J. A. "The Self-Study as a Chariot for Strategic Change." In Ratcliff, J. L., Lubinescu, E., and Gaffney, M. (eds.), *How Accreditation Influences Assessment*. New Directions for Higher Education, no. 113. San Francisco: Jossey-Bass, 2001.

Peters, R. "Accountability and the End(s) of Higher Education." *Change Magazine*, Nov./Dec. 1994, 16–24.

Seymour, D.T. *On Q: Causing Quality in Higher Education*. New York: American Council on Education and Macmillan, 1992.

Sweitzer, K., and Volkwein, J. F. "The Correlates of Prestige Across Graduate and Professional Schools." *Research in Higher Education*, 2009, 50, 129–148.

Volkwein, J. F. "Assessing Institutional Effectiveness and Connecting the Pieces of a Fragmented University." In J. Burke (ed.), *Fixing the Fragmented University*. Bolton, MA: Anker Publishing, 2007.

Volkwein, J. F., and Sweitzer, K. "Institutional Prestige and Reputation Among Research Universities and Liberal Arts Colleges." *Research in Higher Education*, 2006, *47*, 129–148.

Wergin, J. F. "Tasking Responsibility for Student Learning: The Role of Accreditation." *Change*, 2005a, *37*(1), 31–33.

Wergin, J. F. (2005b). "Higher Education: Waking Up to the Importance of Accreditation." *Change*, 2005b, *37*(3), 35–41.

Wolff, R. A. "Accountability and Accreditation: Can Reforms Match Increasing Demands?" In J. C. Burke (ed.), *Achieving Accountability in Higher Education: Balancing Public, Academic, and Market Demands*. San Francisco: Jossey-Bass, 2005.

Recommended Reading

Dodd, A. H. "Accreditation as a Catalyst for Institutional Effectiveness." In M. Dooris, J. Trainer, and W. Kelley (eds.), *Strategic Planning and Institutional Research*. New Directions for Institutional Research, no. 123. San Francisco: Jossey-Bass, 2004.

Massy, W. F. "Measuring Performance: How Colleges and Universities Can Set Meaningful Goals and Be Accountable." In M. W. Peterson (ed.), *ASHE Reader on Planning and Institutional Research*. Needham Heights, MA: Pearson Custom Publishing, 1999.

Middle States Commission on Higher Education. "Student Learning Assessment: Options and Resources." (2nd ed.) Philadelphia: Author, 2007. Retrieved March 6, 2006, from http://www.umes.edu/cms300uploadedFiles/Academic_Affairs/Middle_States/MSCHE%20Student%20Learning%20Assessment.pdf.

North Central Association of Colleges and Schools. *A Handbook of Accreditation*. 2003. Tempe, AZ: North Central Association of Colleges and Schools, Higher Learning Commission. Retrieved April 3, 2009, from http://www.ncahigherlearningcommission.org/download/Handbook03.pdf.

Thomas, A. M. "Consideration of the Resources Needed in an Assessment Program." *NCA Quarterly*, 1991, *66*(2), 430–443.

Volkwein, J. F. "The Four Faces of Institutional Research." In J. F. Volkwein (ed.), *What Is Institutional Research all About: A Critical and Comprehensive Assessment of the Profession*. New Directions for Institutional Research, no. 104. San Francisco: Jossey-Bass, 1999.

J. FREDERICKS VOLKWEIN is emeritus professor of higher education at The Pennsylvania State University and a former director of the Center for the Study of Higher Education.

2

This chapter proposes a model for assessing institutional effectiveness and provides a foundation for the other chapters in this volume.

A Model for Assessing Institutional Effectiveness

J. Fredericks Volkwein

Based on a model of institutional effectiveness, this chapter provides the foundation for the other topics in this volume. Figure 2.1 displays the Volkwein model for assessing institutional effectiveness. The five parts of the model summarize the steps for assessing institutions, programs, faculty, and students.

The first step in the model distinguishes the dual purposes of institutional effectiveness: the *inspirational*, which is oriented toward internal improvement, and the *pragmatic*, which is oriented toward external accountability.

The second step poses five assessment and evaluation questions:

- Are you meeting your goals?
- Are you improving?
- Do you meet professional standards?
- How do you compare to others?
- Are your efforts cost-effective?

These questions (on goal attainment, improvement, meeting standards, benchmarking, and productivity) drive the other steps and lay the groundwork for the research design, data collection, and analysis in steps 3 and 4.

Step 3 is the research design. The appropriate assessment measures and methods vary not only for each of these assessment questions, but also for each of three evaluation levels: institution, program, and individual students

NEW DIRECTIONS FOR INSTITUTIONAL RESEARCH, Assessment Supplement 2009, Spring 2010   © Wiley Periodicals, Inc.
Published online in Wiley InterScience (www.interscience.wiley.com) • DOI: 10.1002/ir.328

Figure 2.1 The Volkwein Model for Assessing Institutional Effectiveness

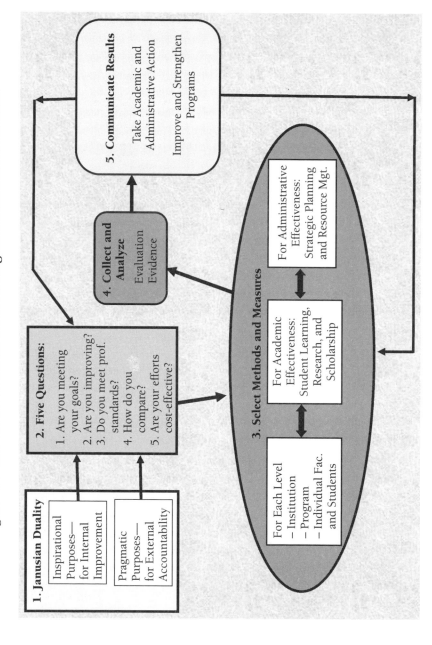

and faculty. Within each of these, assessment strategies vary depending on whether they are designed for demonstrating academic effectiveness or for administrative effectiveness. However, research design is easier when the question being addressed is clear and institution, program, and individual goals are aligned.

Step 4 requires the execution of the research design by collecting, cleaning, and analyzing data and other evaluation evidence. Steps 3 and 4 in the model provide the foundation for Chapters Five through Nine, which focus on assessing basic skills, general education, attainment in the major, personal growth, and alumni outcomes. In addition, Chapters Three and Ten examine some of the data management and measurement issues that need to be addressed in any assessment study.

Step 5 contains the actions that regional and specialized accrediting bodies constantly challenge institutions to do more of: communicate assessment findings and take appropriate action. Alas, most institutions are much better at collecting data than at communicating and acting on them. Chapter Eleven addresses this issue at greater length.

As noted in Chapter 1, the simultaneous and competing needs for both internal improvement and external accountability provide the first foundation for demonstrating institutional and program effectiveness. The second foundation for institutional effectiveness arises from the frequent lack of clarity about assessment purposes and goals.

Five Assessment and Evaluation Questions

Evaluation and assessment force us as professionals to engage in evidence-based thinking, but the nature of the evidence we gather depends on the question asked at the beginning of the process. As suggested in the Volkwein model, institutional effectiveness generally seeks answers to one or more of these generic evaluation questions.

As drivers for assessment activity, each of these questions—goal attainment, improvement, professional standards, comparisons, and cost-effectiveness—has a relevant contribution to make to the overall effectiveness wardrobe (Volkwein, 2004, 2007).

1. *Is the institution or program meeting its goals?* Internal referenced, goal-driven assessment is important and relevant at every level: individual students and faculty, classroom, program, department, and institution. What should students be learning? What are the goals and purposes of this program? Is the university accomplishing its particular mission? Answers require clear, measurable goals and objectives. This formative assessment concentrates on narrowing the gap between goals and actual performance, and thus requires measures or judgments of congruence and incongruence.

2. *Is the institution or program improving?* This improvement-driven self-referenced evaluation compares institutions, programs, and individuals against themselves over time. Formative, self-comparison requires consistent, longitudinal data, or at least time 1 and time 2 data. It recognizes that all institutions and programs are at different starting points, and assumes that every student, faculty member, and program can improve, and identifies how they can improve.

3. *Does the institution or program meet professional standards?* Summative, criterion-referenced evaluation is the traditional accreditation approach and requires assessing institutions, programs, and individuals against criteria established by an external authority. Consequently this criterion-based form of assessment overrides local control and autonomy, and it places a high priority on ensuring minimum levels of competence or performance. It also requires agreement and clarity about the standards and how they are to be measured. Whether applied at the institution, program, or individual level, such assessment usually leads to summative decisions about continuance and discontinuance, acceptability and unacceptability.

4. *How does the institution or program compare to others?* Answering this question requires norm-referenced comparison and benchmarking against peer institutions and programs. Although administrative benchmarking for internal management is now well established, comparison assessment recognizes that institutions and programs are competing, and that many in society like to "keep score" and identify which institution is on top. Using regional and national comparisons has legitimacy with some stakeholders, especially the parents of traditional college students. This explains the interest in *U.S. News and World Report* ratings and rankings, and assumes that competition for faculty and students will drive each institution either to improve or to see its market position deteriorate. Although most campus officials hate the guidebook ratings game, they eagerly follow the performance indicators related to research and scholarly productivity. Whether based on perceived reputation or objective statistics, comparison assessment requires no consensus about performance levels or standards; it merely shows how a college or program stacks up against the competition. As a driver for assessment, comparison measurement requires the selection of appropriate reference groups and common information about them. Grading students "on a curve" is the most common form of such assessment at the classroom level.

5. *Is the institution or program cost-effective?* This is the harsh productivity question and compares costs with benefits, expenditures and

resources with results. Such cost-effectiveness analysis usually requires a degree of professional judgment to go along with the measurement. The costs of higher education constitute an enormous national investment, and universities are under pressure to demonstrate that teaching, research, and service programs are being conducted economically. These external accountability concerns stimulate legislative and trustee interest in class size, faculty workload, administrative salaries, time to degree, loan default, economic impact, and research productivity, among others. Internally, some universities use measures of productivity and performance to assess various administrative and academic support services.

Designing Effectiveness Studies in Higher Education

Four major areas of higher education quality assurance are reflected in the literature:

1. *Classroom, course, and student level:* Assessing the performance, certification, and learning outcomes of individual students

2. *Individual faculty member:* Assessing faculty performance in teaching, scholarship, research, and service

3. *Department and program level:* Reviewing, evaluating, and accrediting academic and administrative programs and services

4. *University or institution level:* Regional accreditation, performance reporting, and governance control

Table 2.1 separates these evaluative focuses into concerns about efficiency and cost versus effectiveness and quality and the major actors with primary, though not exclusive, responsibility at each level. The focus on efficiency and cost occupies the attention of many stakeholders inside and outside the university. As shown in Table 2.1, the responsible actors at each level generally include those who supply the funding to the institution and its faculty and students or those who administer and control those funds after they are received. However, the rest of this chapter examines the influences at work in the right-hand column of Table 2.1: the mechanisms that assess and promote quality and effectiveness at each level of evaluation.

Table 2.1. Levels of Evaluation and Quality Assurance

	Dominant Focus of Evaluation and Primary Responsibility for Quality Assurance	
Levels of Evaluation	Efficiency/Cost	Effectiveness/Quality
Institution	State and local government Boards of trustees	Presidents and chancellors Regional (voluntary) accreditation bodies
Discipline, program, department	Campus financial officers	Professional associations State education departments Campus provosts, deans, faculty
Faculty, researcher, instructor	Federal and foundation grant providers	Federal and foundation review boards Campus provosts, deans, faculty
Student, classroom	Campus financial and enrollment management officers Federal and state financial aid authorities	Faculty State and professional licensure such as for teachers, lawyers, nurses, physicians, accountants, social workers, engineers, architects

Institutional Effectiveness. At the institutional or campus level, presidents or chancellors and trustees are the obvious first line of quality assurance, followed by national and regional accrediting bodies. In addition, the use of externally mandated performance indicators for publicly supported institutions is well established. Early state initiatives to mandate testing have been largely abandoned in favor of less expensive and more practical institutional performance indicators (Ewell, 2005). Borden and Banta (1994) summarized 250 performance indicators in twenty-two categories of input, process, and output. Burke and Serban (1998) examined the indicators used for performance funding in eleven states and found that only 18 percent could be classified as indicators of quality among four-year institutions.

Internally we see an array of management tools that campus leaders have imported to monitor and improve institutional performance. These include the Baldrige Seven Quality Criteria, Six Sigma, and dashboard performance indicators. A growing number of universities, including DePaul, Penn State, Ohio State, Miami University, Tufts, and Illinois State, have developed elaborate scorecards or performance dashboards to track and monitor their own progress and effectiveness compared to a group of peers. In their study of performance dashboards, Terkla, Wiseman, and Cohen (2005) report eleven broad categories of indicators, with one to five subgroups containing six to one hundred different indicators in each subgroup.

New Directions for Institutional Research • DOI: 10.1002/ir

The largest numbers of these dashboard indicators reflect measures of admissions, enrollments, faculty and student profiles, and finances, including tuition, employee compensation, financial aid and fellowships, endowment, alumni giving, and Moody's ratings of financial health. Institutions are struggling to add indicators of academic and student outcomes performance, but few have gotten beyond retention and graduation rates; degrees awarded; class size; student-to-faculty ratios; honors and study abroad participation; student, faculty, and alumni satisfaction; research funding, expenditures, and patents; employment and graduate school attendance by graduates; library rankings; and reputational ratings. Of course, many of these are indicators that the public associates with quality, but we know from the meta-analysis by Pascarella and Terenzini (2005) that these reflect only indirectly on students' actual educational experiences and learning outcomes.

As discussed in Chapter One, the elaborate regional accreditation process provides quality assurance based on self-review and peer assessment by the member institutions of the six regions: Middle States, New England, North Central, Northwest, Southern, and Western. Perhaps the most dramatic change in these reviews is illustrated in Figure 2.2. Accreditation reviews have shifted substantially away from the earlier focus on standards for inputs and resources, and toward judging institutional effectiveness from measurable outcomes. This paradigm shift is not complete since some attention is still directed toward institutional and academic inputs, processes, and outputs, but in most cases evidence of student learning and other outcomes is increasingly expected to be the centerpiece of the effectiveness review, and using that evidence to improve is viewed to be the hallmark of a healthy learning organization.

Peter Ewell (2005) has described the history of accreditation and state policy attempts to establish institution-centered assessment in higher education. Unfortunately, these attempts have received variable levels of institutional and faculty cooperation. There are a few model institutions like SUNY Albany and UC Davis that have conducted institution level assessments and posted the findings for all to see, and institutions increasingly post their accreditation self-studies on their web sites as Volkwein recommends (2004, 2007).

Department and Program Effectiveness. At the program level, the picture is less complicated. There are two major types of program evaluation: program review internally and program accreditation externally. Both contribute to institutional effectiveness.

Specialized academic and vocational accrediting bodies and professional societies scrutinize and accredit officially recognized programs in an array of specialties. This quality assurance activity began in some of the most mature disciplines like medicine, law, engineering, and theology and now includes nearly one hundred fields of study, ranging from accounting to music, chemistry to journalism, librarianship to nursing, forestry to

Figure 2.2. Evolving Focus of Academic Quality and Effectiveness

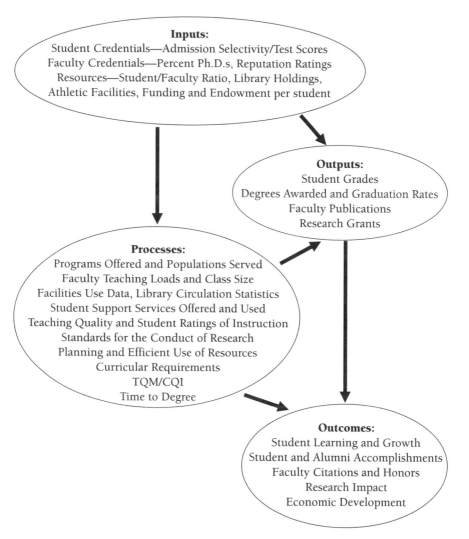

physical therapy, and public administration to teacher education. Institutions are eager to meet the standards set by these professional organizations because accredited programs attract the best students, as well as federal, foundation, and state funding.

A number of scholars in higher education (Barak and Mets, 1995; Banta, Lund, Black, and Oblander, 1996) maintain that the most effective form of institutional assessment and improvement is the campus-based program review. This conclusion is reinforced by various accreditation bodies that for the past decade have called on institutions and programs to create a culture of evidence that promotes academic self-renewal.

NEW DIRECTIONS FOR INSTITUTIONAL RESEARCH • DOI: 10.1002/ir

Even in the absence of external accreditors, most campuses have their own provost-led and faculty-endorsed program review processes. Campus strategic plans depend on realistic assessments of internal strengths and weaknesses matched against external constraints and opportunity. Consequently nearly every university has developed its own program review and quality control measures, often coordinating these internal reviews with those of the specialized disciplines and professions. Program reviews under ideal conditions are integrated into the fabric of academic affairs and constitute a constructive process of self-examination and continuous improvement. This is sometimes accomplished by a university-wide council that reviews publicly all institutional reviews. The University of California at Santa Barbara and Florida International University appear to have such a model review process now, and the State University of New York at Albany had one in the 1970s and 1980s. In addition, many states have mandated periodic reviews of academic programs, especially at the graduate level. Sometimes these are coordinated with and draw on, rather than override, the internal and external academic program review processes described here.

Most universities seem to have an unending stream of self-study documents and site visit teams from regional, state, and discipline-based bodies. But at least these accreditation groups focus mostly on educational effectiveness rather than on the latest guidebook ratings and expenditures per student. Hence, accreditation bodies are educational allies rather than enemies. Program reviews are discussed more thoroughly in Chapter Four.

Faculty Effectiveness. At the individual level, faculty research and scholarly performance has for decades been peer-reviewed by federal grant agencies, foundation and industry sponsors, and journal editors and book publishers, among others. At the campus level, annual reports of faculty activity have been a long tradition, and these increasingly focus on instructional, research, and scholarly productivity rather than mere activity. In addition, most institutions use annual reviews of faculty productivity in order to make merit pay decisions.

Assessing faculty effectiveness has changed dramatically since the publication of Boyer's 1990 perspectives on the four domains of scholarship: the scholarship of discovery, the scholarship of application, the scholarship of teaching, and the scholarship of integration. Boyer has reshaped our thinking about how faculty teaching, research, and service activities are connected and integrated. John Braxton (2006) and his colleagues summarize what we have learned about the impact of Boyer's four domains. The majority of doctoral, master's, and baccalaureate institutions have developed a more complex, nuanced view of scholarship that incorporates many aspects of teaching and service and integration of knowledge. Moreover, many campuses have reshaped the faculty evaluation and academic rewards structure in ways that align not only with Boyer's domains, but also with differential institutional mission (see especially the chapters in Braxton,

NEW DIRECTIONS FOR INSTITUTIONAL RESEARCH • DOI: 10.1002/ir

2006). Consequently, Boyer's thinking has reduced university fragmentation and promoted integration.

In addition to Boyer's influence, an array of national bodies and higher education scholars have expressed concerns about the state of undergraduate education in research universities. Led by Chickering and Gamson (1987), the American Association for Higher Education (1992) published seven principles of good educational practice aimed at influencing faculty instructional behavior. This was followed by the National Center for Higher Education Management Systems' twelve characteristics of effective instruction (Ewell and Jones, 1996).

Responding to these national concerns, some research universities, like Penn State, adopted policies calling not only for student evaluations of instruction in every course each semester, but also for periodic posttenure evaluations of faculty performance that document faculty accomplishments in teaching, research and creative work, professional activity, and university or public service. Many research universities have developed rather elaborate systems of faculty evaluation. For example, in the University of California System, this faculty assessment is linked to decisions about merit pay and steps within rank and takes place every two or three years for each ladder faculty member, including tenured faculty. Faculty teaching performance is to be evaluated by students at the end of each course each quarter. Individual instructors and individual departments can vary the survey items and teaching dimensions that are assessed, but most assessments include the overall rating of the instructor and the overall rating of the course. These student evaluations are complemented by faculty peer evaluations of teaching that include classroom observations at the point of preparation for promotion and merit review. At the University of California at its Santa Barbara and at Davis campuses, these processes seem especially well conducted. While research achievement is given priority over teaching, the great majority of the administrators, faculty committee chairs, and deans emphasize the prominence of the teaching performance record in personnel decisions, and the university documents and Web sites describe an array of teaching and instructional resources. These healthy changes seem especially effective because they include participation by faculty governance.

Assessing Students. At the student and classroom level, the picture is more complicated than at the program level. The needs of students and the areas of their learning vary highly among institutions and degree programs. Students are diverse, and the dimensions of the learning processes in American higher education are complex. Assessing student performance is also complex and hence difficult to summarize for institutional performance.

A map of this complex outcomes terrain was first developed by Astin, Panos, and Creager (1967). Their conceptual scheme organizes college outcomes by three dimensions: type of outcome, type of data, and time. They divide outcomes into cognitive and affective (or noncognitive) and data into

Table 2.2. Classification of Student Outcomes by Type of Outcome and Type of Data

	Outcome	
Data	Affective	Cognitive
Psychological	Attitudes and values	Basic skills
	Educational and career goals	General education and critical thinking skills
	Satisfaction	Knowledge in the major
	Personal and social growth	Intellectual growth and academic performance (grade point average)
Behavioral	Choice of major	Educational attainment
	Choice of career	Occupational attainment
	Student-body leadership	
	Community leadership	

psychological and behavioral (or observable). The time dimension consists of outcomes that occur during college (time 1) and after college (time 2). Tables 2.2 and 2.3 provide examples. For the purposes of this volume, we discuss the cognitive outcomes, mostly but not entirely, in Chapters Five through Seven: basic skills, general education, and attainment of the major, respectively. Chapter Eight highlights the affective or noncognitive outcomes. In Chapter Three, Patrick Terenzini discusses all of these and presents his own conceptual framework. Chapter Nine on alumni studies focuses on outcomes that occur after college (Table 2.3). Although most chapters in this volume discuss assessment challenges, Chapter Ten examines our "top ten" measurement problems.

Table 2.3. Examples of Measures Representing Different Times, Types of Data, and Outcomes

Type of Outcome	Type of Data	Time 1 (During College)	Time 2 (After College)
Affective	Psychological	Satisfaction with college	Job satisfaction
Affective	Behavioral	Participation in student government or service organizations	Participation in political or community service organizations
Cognitive	Psychological	Graduate Record Exam scores and admissions tests for medicine, law, business, engineering	Test scores for certification in medicine, law, accounting, civil engineering, teaching
Cognitive	Behavioral	Persistence in college and degree completion	Advancement in career and income

Most American higher education scholars think of assessment in the following ways:

Assessment is the systematic gathering, interpretations, and use of information about student learning for purposes of improvement [Marchese, 1997, p. 79].

Assessment tends to be locally designed and executed evaluation research intended to determine the effects of a college or university on its students, centered on learning outcomes, for the purpose of improving teaching and learning [AAHE Assessment Forum, 1992].

Student Outcomes Assessment is the act of assembling and analyzing both qualitative and quantitative teaching and learning outcomes evidence in order to examine their congruence with an institution's stated purposes and educational objectives [Middle States, 1996].

Each of these definitions suggests that student outcomes assessment is goal driven, empirically based, and improvement oriented. I always tell my students that assessment is a process, not a product, and a beginning, not an end.

Traditionally student performance and learning are evaluated where learning primarily takes place: in the classroom, where faculty and students interact. However, the twentieth-century testing movement made it possible to ensure minimum standards by requiring particular levels of performance on standardized examinations. These performance standards now range from college entrance tests (like the SAT and ACT exams), to tests of student basic skills (like College BASE, or a foreign language proficiency test), general education skills (such as the ACT Collegiate Assessment of Academic Proficiency and the ETS Measure of Academic Proficiency and Progress), and attainment in the major (such as the ETS major field exams). On graduation, individual students may face not only graduate school entrance tests, but also assessments of their qualifications to become a practicing professional in many fields like accounting (CPA exam), law (state bar exam), engineering (Fundamentals of Engineering and Professional Engineering exams), medicine (medical boards), and teaching (PRAXIS). We examine each of these more thoroughly in the upcoming chapters.

Since standardized tests may or may not fit the goals, curricula, or needs of particular institutions and programs, the field has developed an array of other assessment strategies for measuring student learning outcomes (Volkwein, 2004; Tebo-Messina and Prus, 1995). These are some of the other most common assessment sources of evidence, and each has its advantages, as we will discuss in subsequent chapters:

• Locally developed comprehensive exams (including essays)
• Appraisals of student performances, exhibits, and simulations

- Written surveys and questionnaires of student attitudes, values, and experiences
- Student self-evaluations of abilities, skills, and gains
- Senior thesis or research projects
- Capstone courses
- Interviews
- External examiners
- Analysis of transcripts, archival records, and course content
- Portfolios
- Behavioral observations (including internships)
- Classroom research and course-embedded assessments
- Alumni studies and placement data

Although these various assessment strategies may be quite useful for assessing one type of student learning or another, each of these approaches (except perhaps alumni outcomes) shares the disadvantage of being not very useful reflections of educational effectiveness for the institution as a whole. Even standardized tests have limited usefulness. Although they may be appropriate for particular areas of knowledge in the major, such tests are not regarded as good ways to measure complex thinking, communication skills, teamwork, or ethical reasoning. Hence, it is very difficult to aggregate the results of student learning assessment up to the institution level. This measurement challenge provides a practical obstacle to using student outcomes assessment for institutional effectiveness.

To overcome this obstacle, some universities have divided their assessment activities into decentralized efforts that focus on assessing outcomes for individual students versus centralized efforts that assess the outcomes of large populations of undergraduates (Volkwein, 2007). This more centralized approach relies heavily on the collection of self-reported student experiences, involvement, skills, and gains in knowledge. The use of self-reported measures to describe and assess the relative differences among large groups of students and alumni is now widespread (Kuh, 2005). Under the right conditions, student self-reports are both valid and reliable, especially for measuring the outcomes for groups of students rather than individuals. (Chapter Ten discusses the adequacy of self-reported measures at greater length.)

Moreover, there now are a couple of decades of studies indicating that student engagement, involvement, and effort are strongly associated with positive outcomes like student learning. Since the conditions that foster student learning are easier to measure than student learning itself, recent studies have focused on involvement, commitment, engagement, effort, and good educational practices as the more easily measured outcomes (Kuh, Pace, and Vesper, 1997; Kuh, 2001; Pascarella et al., 2006; Porter, 2006; Volkwein, 2007). Such research has spawned the use of a large number of instruments and scales for measuring student experiences and gains.

Reviewed in Chapter Eight, these include the ACT College Outcomes Survey, College Student Experiences Questionnaire, National Survey of Student Engagement, HERI College Student Survey, and an array of institution-specific and discipline-specific instruments.

Thus, we have a complicated collage of evaluation and assessment challenges for institutions, programs, faculty, and students. The faculty mostly assesses individual students by assigning them grades in individual courses. Rarely are undergraduate students evaluated holistically. Provosts, deans, and chairs mostly evaluate faculty individually and most thoroughly at the points of promotion and tenure. Federal and foundation sponsors, as well as publishers and editors, also focus on particular manuscripts and particular research proposals of particular faculty. Rarely is a faculty member's contribution to institutional and program goal attainment a matter of documented review. Program reviews are widespread, including both formative internal reviews and summative external reviews by specialized accreditors. The variety and complexity and typical focus of these program, faculty, and student assessments are enormous, hence contributing to university fragmentation and presenting assessment researchers with daunting challenges.

References

American Association for Higher Education. *Nine Principles of Good Practice for Assessing Student Learning.* 1992. Retrieved March 6, 2006, from http://www.cord.edu/dept/assessment/nineprin.pdf.

Astin, A. W., Panos, R. J., and Creager, J. A. *National Norms for Entering College Freshmen—Fall 1966.* Washington, DC: American Council on Education, 1967.

Banta, T. W., Lund, J. P., Black, K. E., and Oblander, F. W. (eds). *Assessment in Practice: Putting Principles to Work on College Campuses.* San Francisco: Jossey-Bass, 1996.

Barak, R. J., and Mets, L. A. (eds.). *Using Academic Program Review.* New Directions for Institutional Research, no. 86. San Francisco: Jossey-Bass, 1995.

Borden, V. M., and Banta, T. W. (eds.). *Using Performance Indicators to Guide Strategic Decision Making.* New Directions for Institutional Research, no. 82. San Francisco: Jossey-Bass, 1994.

Boyer, E. L. *Scholarship Reconsidered: Priorities of the Professoriate.* Princeton NJ: Carnegie Foundation for the Advancement of Teaching, 1990.

Braxton, J. (ed.). *Analyzing Faculty Work and Rewards Through Boyer's Four Domains of Scholarship.* New Directions for Institutional Research, no. 129. San Francisco: Jossey-Bass, 2006.

Burke, J. C., and Serban, A. M. (eds.). *Performance Funding for Public Higher Education: Fad or Trend?* New Directions for Institutional Research, no. 97. San Francisco: Jossey-Bass, 1998.

Chickering, A. W., and Gamson, Z. F. "Seven Principles for Good Practices in Undergraduate Education." *AAHE Bulletin,* 1987, *39*(7), 3–7.

Ewell, P. T. "Can Assessment Serve Accountability? It Depends on the Question." In J. Burke (ed.), *Achieving Accountability in Higher Education: Balancing Public, Academic, and Market Demands.* San Francisco: Jossey Bass, 2005.

Ewell, P. T., and Jones, D. P. *Indicators of "Good Practice" in Undergraduate Education: A Handbook for Development and Implementation.* Boulder, CO: National Center for Higher Education Management Systems, 1996.

NEW DIRECTIONS FOR INSTITUTIONAL RESEARCH • DOI: 10.1002/ir

Kuh, G. D. "Imagine Asking the Client: Using Student and Alumni Surveys for Accountability in Higher Education." In J. Burke (ed.), *Achieving Accountability in Higher Education: Balancing Public, Academic, and Market Demands.* San Francisco: Jossey-Bass,
2005.

Kuh, G. D. "Assessing What Really Matters to Student Learning: Inside the National Survey of Student Engagement." *Change,* 2001, *33*(3), 10–17, 66.

Kuh, G. D., Pace, C. R., and Vesper, N. "The Development of Process Indicators to Estimate Student Gains Associated with Good Practices in Undergraduate Education."
Research in Higher Education, 1997, *38*(4), 435–454.

Marchese, T. J. "The New Conversations About Learning: Insights from Neuroscience
and Anthropology, Cognitive Science and Work-Place Studies." In Assessing Impact:
Evidence and Action. Proceedings from the 1997 AAHE Assessment Conference.
Washington, DC: American Association for Higher Education, 1997.

Middle States Commission on Higher Education. "Framework for Outcomes Assessment." (2nd ed.) Philadelphia: Author, 1996.

Pascarella, E. T., Cruce, T., Umbach, P. D., Wolniak, G. C., Kuh, G. D., Carini, R. M.,
et al. "Institutional Selectivity and Good Practices in Undergraduate Education: How
Strong Is the Link?" *Journal of Higher Education,* 2006, 77, 251–285.

Pascarella, E. T., and Terenzini, P. T. *How College Affects Students: A Third Decade of
Research.* San Francisco: Jossey-Bass, 2005.

Porter, S. R. "Institutional Structures and Student Engagement." *Research in Higher Education,* 2006, 47, 521–558.

Tebo-Messina, M., and Prus, J. "Assessing General Education: An Overview of Methods." Paper presented at the American Association for Higher Education 10th Annual
Conference on Assessment & Quality, Boston, MA, 1995.

Terkla, D., Wiseman, M., and Cohen, M. "Institutional Dashboards: Navigational Tool
for Colleges and Universities." Paper presented at the 27th Annual EAIR Forum, Riga,
Latvia, Aug. 2005.

Volkwein, J. F (ed.). "Assessing Student Learning in the Major: What's the Question?"
In B. Keith (ed.), *Contexts for Learning: Institutional Strategies for Managing Curricular Change Through Assessment.* Stillwater, OK: New Forums Press, 2004.

Volkwein, J. F. "Assessing Institutional Effectiveness and Connecting the Pieces of a
Fragmented University." In J. Burke (ed.), *Fixing the Fragmented University.* Bolton,
MA: Anker, 2007.

Recommended Reading

Astin, A. W. *Achieving Educational Excellence: A Critical Assessment of Priorities and Practices in Higher Education.* San Francisco: Jossey-Bass, 1985.

Banta, T. W., and Associates. *Building a Scholarship of Assessment.* San Francisco: Jossey-
Bass, 2002.

Borden, V. M., and Williams, J. "Developing Credible and Meaningful Performance Indicators." Paper presented at the AIR Forum, Tampa, FL, May 2003.

Boyer Commission on Educating Undergraduates in the Research University. "Reinventing Undergraduate Education: A Blueprint for America's Research Universities."
1998. Retrieved February 28, 2006, from http://naples.cc.sunysb.edu/Pres/boyer.nsf/
673918d46fbf653e852565ec0056ff3e/d955b61ffddd590a852565ec005717ae/$FILE/
boyer.pdf.

Burke, J. C., and Minassians, H. P. (eds.). *Reporting Higher Education Results: Missing
Links in the Performance Chain.* New Directions for Institutional Research, no. 116.
San Francisco: Jossey-Bass, 2002.

Etzioni, A. "Administrative and Professional Authority." In M. C. Brown II (ed.), *Organization and Governance in Higher Education*. Boston: Pearson Custom Publishing, 2000.

Hu, S., Kuh, G. D., and Gayles, J. G. "Undergraduate Research Experiences: Are Students at Research Universities Advantaged?" Paper presented at the annual meeting of American Educational Research Association, Montreal, Canada, April 2005.

Ikenberry, S. O., and Friedman, R. C. *Beyond Academic Departments*. San Francisco: Jossey-Bass, 1972.

Jacobi, M., Astin, A., and Ayala, F. *College Student Outcomes Assessment: A Talent Development Perspective*. ASHE-ERIC Higher Education Report, no. 7. Washington, DC: Association for the Study of Higher Education, 1987.

Palomba, C., and Banta, T. W. *Assessment Essentials: Planning, Implementing, and Improving Assessment in Higher Education*. San Francisco: Jossey-Bass, 1999.

Pascarella, E. T., and Terenzini, P. T. *How College Affects Students: Findings and Insights from Twenty Years of Research*. San Francisco: Jossey-Bass, 1991.

Schneider, C. "Involving Faculty Members in Assessment." *Liberal Education*, 1988, 74(3), 2–4.

Seymour, D. T. *On Q: Causing Quality in Higher Education*. New York: American Council on Education and Macmillan, 1992.

Shirley, R., and Volkwein, J. F. "Establishing Academic Program Priorities." *Journal of Higher Education*, 1978, 49(5), 472–488.

Stark, J., and Lowther, M. *Strengthening the Ties that Bind: Integrating Undergraduate Liberal and Professional Study*. Ann Arbor: Professional Preparation Network, University of Michigan, 1988.

Strauss, L. C., and Volkwein, J. F. "Predictors of Student Commitment at Two-Year and Four-Year Institutions." *Journal of Higher Education*, 2004, 75, 203–227.

Volkwein, J. F. (ed.). *What Is Institutional Research all About? A Critical and Comprehensive Assessment of the Profession*. New Directions for Institutional Research, no. 104. San Francisco: Jossey-Bass, 1999.

Volkwein, J. F., Lattuca, L. R., Harper, B. J., and Domingo, R. J. "The Impact of Accreditation on Student Experiences and Learning Outcomes." *Research in Higher Education*, 2007, 48, 129–148.

Volkwein, J. F., and Sweitzer, K. "Institutional Prestige and Reputation Among Research Universities and Liberal Arts Colleges." *Research in Higher Education*, 2006, 47, 129–148.

Walvoord, B. E. *Assessment Clear and Simple: A Practical Guide for Institutions, Departments and General Education*. San Francisco: Jossey-Bass, 2004.

Western Association of Schools and Colleges. "WASC 2001 Handbook of Accreditation." 2001. Alameda, CA: Author. Retrieved March 6, 2006, from http://www.wascsenior .org/wasc/Doc_Lib/2001%20Handbook.pdf.

J. FREDERICKS VOLKWEIN is emeritus professor of higher education at The Pennsylvania State University and a former director of the Center for the Study of Higher Education.

3

This chapter is reprinted from the Journal of Higher
Education, *1989, by permission of Ohio State
University Press.*

Assessment with Open Eyes: Pitfalls in Studying Student Outcomes

Patrick T. Terenzini

There can be little doubt that "assessment" is here to stay. At least seven
national reports have appeared [between 1984 and 1989, when this article
first appeared], all critical of higher education in America and all giving a
central role to "assessment"—the measurement of the educational impact
of an institution on its students. At least eleven states have adopted formal
assessment requirements (Ewell, 1987a), as many more are moving in that
direction, and regional accrediting associations are writing student outcomes assessment activities into their reaccreditation requirements.

The fact that the origins of the push toward assessment are external to
most campuses is significant. Surveys indicate that while "over 50 percent
of college administrators support assessing general education, . . . only 15
percent report doing anything about it. In the more complex area of 'value-
added' assessment, some 65 percent support the concept but less than 10
percent are fielding value-added programs" (Ewell, 1987a, p. 25). The clear
implication of these findings is that for many colleges and universities,
assessment is a relatively new undertaking: they are either just beginning
to explore and implement assessment programs, or they have not yet even
begun.

In fact, through such activities as course examinations, senior comprehensive examinations, periodic program evaluations, or some types of student, alumni, and employer surveys, many campuses have been engaged in
"assessment," by one definition or another, for some time. These efforts,
however, are typically undertaken by individuals or by individual offices

NEW DIRECTIONS FOR INSTITUTIONAL RESEARCH, Assessment Supplement 2009, Spring 2010   © Wiley Periodicals, Inc.
Published online in Wiley InterScience (www.interscience.wiley.com) • DOI: 10.1002/ir.329

or committees and are not coordinated in any way. Nor are they part of any comprehensive, institutional plan for ongoing, systematic self-study and improvement. Much of the discussion that follows will be useful to such discrete, individual assessment activities (for example, a department's evaluation of its courses or programs), but because the major thrust of state boards or agencies and regional accrediting bodies is for systematic, campus-wide assessment activities, this chapter focuses on potential problems in the development of institution-wide assessment programs.

Moreover, as Astin (1985) has pointed out, we have for years tended to think of undergraduate program "quality" as synonymous with "resources invested." The "best" colleges and universities are frequently thought to be those with high-ability and high-achieving students, more books in their library, more faculty with terminal degrees, lower student-faculty ratios, larger endowments, and so on. Although a reasonable argument can be made that undergraduate program quality and resources invested are not independent, the increased emphasis on assessment has radically altered the nature of discussions of undergraduate program quality. Increasingly, claims to quality must be based not on resources or processes but on outcomes. The benefits to institutions and students of this reformulation of the issues are substantial. Because they are detailed elsewhere, however (for example, Ewell, 1984; Rossmann and El-Khawas, 1987), the major ones will be only suggested here.

Perhaps most important, assessment requires a redirection of institutional attention from resources to education. Now that the costs of a college education are identifiable and measurable, important people (for example, legislators, parents, students) now want to know what the return is on their investments. What does one get out of a college education? The question forces a fundamental introspection on the part of both individual faculty members and institutions. Assessment requires reconsideration of the essential purposes and expected academic and nonacademic outcomes of a college education. It also requires a clarity of institutional and programmatic purpose, as well as a specificity of practice often absent on many campuses or hidden in the generalities of recruiting materials. What should students get out of attending college? What should they get out of attending *this* college? In addition, assessment requires that we try to understand whether the things we do and believe to be educational in fact produce the intended outcomes.

These are all substantial benefits. Many campuses, however, fail to recognize them, instead viewing assessment as merely one more external reporting obligation, as something to be done as quickly and as painlessly as possible. When assessment is seen in this light, significant opportunities to enhance educational programs are likely to be lost.

But though advice on how assessment programs should be designed and implemented is easy to come by, the pitfalls of assessment are more obscure, typically treated only cursorily (if at all) in the literature. This chapter calls attention to some of those pitfalls and suggests, however briefly, how at least some of them might be avoided. The chapter is not intended to discourage institutions from developing assessment programs. On the contrary, its purpose is twofold: first, to identify some of the serious conceptual, measurement, organizational, and political problems likely to be encountered in the process of designing and implementing an assessment program; and second, by identifying some of the pitfalls, to help people who are involved in assessment to ".do" it well. To accomplish these purposes, the chapter focuses on three major areas: (1) definitional issues, (2) organizational and implementational issues, and (3) methodological issues.

Definitional Issues

One of the most significant and imposing obstacles to the advancement of the assessment agenda at the national level is the absence of any consensus on precisely what *assessment* means. Some have used the term to mean testing individual student achievement levels in various academic areas. To others it means a review of the general education program and an evaluation of whether students are receiving a "liberal education." To still others it means a series of surveys of current students, alumni, or even employers, undertaken for program evaluation and planning purposes. And to still others, it means nothing less than institution-wide self-study, applicable to teaching, research, service, and administrative and management functions. Lack of clarity about exactly what this term means on a campus constitutes a significant threat to the success of any assessment effort.

In thinking about what "assessment" can mean, it is useful to keep three questions in mind, for the answers will have a powerful influence on the kind of assessment in which a campus becomes involved, as well as on the issues and problems it will face. The first question is: "What is the purpose of the assessment?" Why is the assessment program being designed? Although something of an oversimplification, the answers to this question generally fall into one (or both) of two categories: assessment for the enhancement of teaching and learning or assessment for purposes of accountability to some organizationally higher authority, whether internal or external to an institution. The answers to this question parallel the purposes of formative and summative evaluation: the first is intended to guide program modification and improvement, while the second is undertaken to inform some final judgment about worth or value.

The second question is: "What is to be the level of assessment?" Who is to be assessed? Will the assessment focus on individual students, where the information gathered on each student is inherently interesting? Or will it focus on groups, where individual information is aggregated to summarize some characteristic of the group (for example, average performance on some measure)? In this instance, "group" refers to any of a wide variety of student aggregations, such as at the course, program, department, college or school, campus, or system level; or to students grouped by sex, race/ethnicity, class year, major, place of residence, or whatever.

The third question is: "What is to be assessed?" On which of a variety of possible educational outcomes will assessment efforts be focused? Several "outcomes" taxonomies are available (for example, Bloom, Englehart, Furst, Hill, and Krathwohl, 1956; Bowen, 1977; Krathwohl, Bloom, and Masia, 1964; Lenning, 1979). A simple yet useful general typology has been given by Ewell (1987a, 1987b), who suggests four basic dimensions of outcomes: (1) knowledge (both breadth and depth) outcomes, (2) skills outcomes (including basic, higher-order, and career-related skills), (3) attitudes and values outcomes (frequently overlooked), and (4) behavioral outcomes (what students do, both during and after college). If these three questions are juxtaposed in a three-dimensional matrix such as Figure 3.1, one can begin to see how varying approaches to assessment can be categorized.

Some would assert that assessment in its purest form has the improvement of learning and teaching as its primary purpose and that it focuses on individual students. In this approach, most notably practiced at Alverno College, but also at King's College in Pennsylvania and Clayton State College in Georgia, analysis of individual student performance is an integral part of the teaching and learning process. Students receive regular feedback on their knowledge and skill development, and teachers use the same infor-

Figure 3.1. Terenzini's Assessment Taxonomy

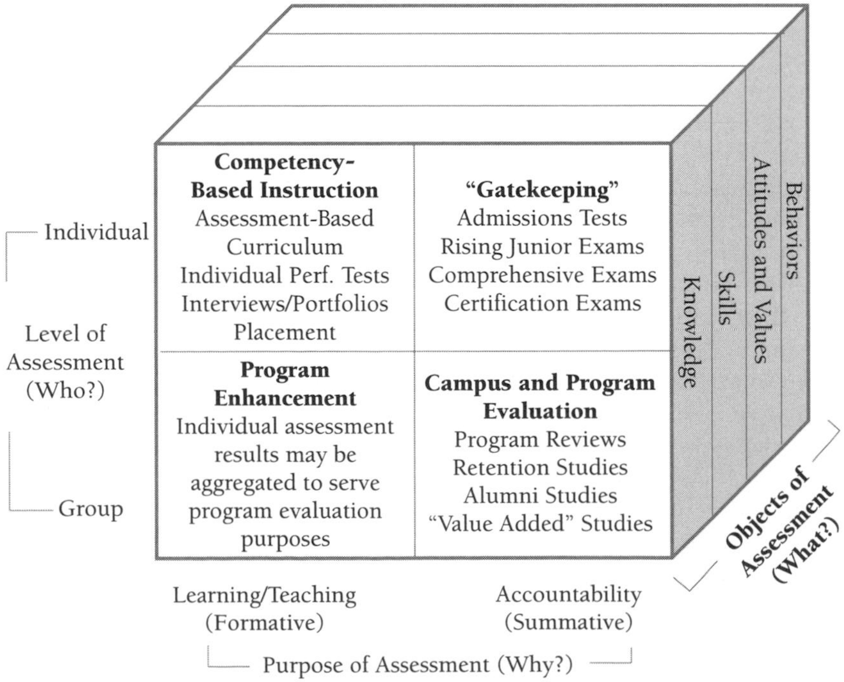

mation to shape their teaching strategies, activities, and styles, as well as to guide individual student learning.

Some other standard assessment practices also fall in this category. For example, placement examinations and other diagnostic measures are clearly teaching and learning focused at the individual level. They are intended to determine a student's learning readiness and to permit assignment of the student to the most beneficial learning sequence (for example, developmental studies or honors programs).

Individual assessment results may, of course, be aggregated to evaluate program effectiveness where the evaluation is intended to be formative, facilitating program modifications and increased effectiveness. (The multiple, often overlapping uses of assessment data mean that the lines between the cells in Figure 3.1 are rather permeable.) For example, assessments of general education program outcomes might fall in this category, unless of course the major purpose of such an assessment is for accountability purposes (that is, summative).

Moving to the right-hand column of Figure 3.1, one can note that assessment programs with a clear accountability orientation can be of two varieties. At the individual level, assessment serves a gatekeeping function, sifting and sorting the qualified from the unqualified. This category includes such practices as admissions testing (for example, ACT, SAT, and others) and "rising junior" examinations employed in Florida, Georgia, and elsewhere. Other varieties of the accountability-oriented conception of assessment include comprehensive examinations in the student's academic major field (a practice enjoying a revival) and certification examinations in professional fields (for example, nursing).

These latter sorts of examinations may, of course, also serve accountability assessment purposes at the group level. Assessment programs comprising this group-accountability cell focus on group mean scores rather than on individual scores. The principal interest is in program enhancement, in determining the level of effectiveness or quality at which a program, department, school, or entire campus is functioning. Assessment activities in this cell include academic program reviews, analysis of student attrition rates and reasons, alumni follow-up studies, and various forms of "value-added" assessment. The focus or purpose is primarily evaluative and administrative, and the information so obtained may be used for accounting to external bodies, although it may also be highly useful for internal program improvement and planning and for enhancing teaching and learning.

Each institution must decide for itself, consistent with its mission, what the character of its assessment program is to be on each of these three dimensions (and for subsets within these major categories). The point here is the importance of being clear on a more-or-less campus-wide basis about why assessment is being undertaken, who is to be assessed, and what educational outcomes are to be assessed. Time spent in committee work and in other forms of public discussion of these three questions will be time extremely well spent. An inadequate conceptual foundation for an assessment program will produce confusion, anxiety, and more heat than light.

Organizational and Implementational Issues

Assuming some reasonable level of agreement is reached on the purposes and objects of assessment, it is important to keep always in mind that institutional change is embedded in any conception of assessment. Depending on where the changes occur and how they are managed, they can produce higher levels of individual and organizational performance and pride in accomplishment, or they can produce internal insurrection. Several significant organizational and implementational hazards must be addressed at the outset.

Mobilizing Support. A vital and difficult task involves enlisting the support of concerned parties. The active and visible support of senior executive officers (particularly the president and chief academic officer) is absolutely necessary but, unfortunately, not sufficient. Faculty support is also needed, and without it prospects for a successful assessment program are dim. According to Ewell (1984), faculty objections are likely to come from either or both of two sources: first, the fear of being negatively evaluated, and second, a philosophical opposition based on the belief that the outcomes of college are inherently unmeasurable and that the evidence from such studies is "misleading, oversimplifying, or inaccurate" (p. 73).

If sufficient attention has been given to public discussion and review of the program's purposes and objects, much will already have been done to allay the fears of faculty members and others. Assessment, even when required by an external body, should be seen by all as a developmental, not punitive, undertaking. It should be a vehicle for individual and institutional improvement, not a search for documentation on which to evaluate individual faculty members, or to cut budgets, or retrench programs. Indeed, in some institutions (for example, in Tennessee and at Northeast Missouri State University), it is used not as a basis for withdrawing departmental support but for increasing it, whether to reward good work or to help a unit improve. Some basic level of trust must be established, and good-faith participation in assessment activities should not be discouraged.

Ewell (1988) recommends being publicly clear about what an assessment program is not intended to do. This would include a clear and public specification of what data are to be collected, by whom, for what purposes, the conditions under which the data will be made available, and to whom they will be available. Northeast Missouri State University (1984), one of the assessment pioneers, recommends against using assessment data to support negative decisions, and Rossmann and El-Khawas (1987) caution against mixing assessment procedures with faculty evaluation procedures. Rossmann and El-Khawas also recommend sensitivity to the timing of the initiation of assessment efforts. If a financial crisis, retrenchment, or major reorganization is imminent (or underway), individual and unit anxiety levels may already be high enough without introducing a potentially threatening program.

Yanikoski (1987) has suggested thinking and speaking in terms of "progress assessment" rather than "outcomes assessment." The switch can be important symbolically as well as conceptually. "Assessing outcomes" implies a certain finality: that a summative evaluation and judgment are to be made, that the "bottom line" is about to be drawn. "Assessing progress," by contrast, implies an ongoing, formative process, which, in turn, suggests that time remains to make any necessary improvements. The whole tone of "progress assessment" is more positive, less threatening.

Faculty reservations about the measurability of outcomes must also be addressed, and several approaches are possible. One powerful way to allay faculty concerns about evaluation and the measurability of student progress is to include faculty in the design and implementation of the process and especially in the interpretation of results and development of recommendations. Respected faculty opinion leaders should be involved, and faculty members with technical specialties in research design, measurement, and other important areas should be recruited as consultants. Faculty members on most campuses constitute a significant, but untapped, source of technical and political support for an assessment effort.

Another way to ease concerns about the measurability of student progress is to ensure that multiple measures are incorporated into one's assessment program. The concept of triangulation in astronomy, surveying and map reading, and of successive approximations in probability theory are familiar to most faculty members. Multitrait, multimethod matrices can be highly useful, arraying in the rows those content and skill areas to be assessed and, across the columns, the assessment techniques and approaches that might be used to assess each trait. One can then judge the extent to which each assessment area will be covered by multiple measures. Adoption of multiple measures is likely to have a face validity that will appeal to faculty members as well as increase the confidence that can be placed in interpretations of the data. The psychometric importance of using multiple measures is discussed further below.

Whatever approach is taken, however, everyone involved must recognize that judgments of program and institutional quality are made all the time by many different people. The issue is not really whether "assessments" should be made, but rather what is to be the nature, sources, and quality of the evidence on which those judgments are based.

Finally, assessment programs that start small, perhaps on a pilot basis, are more likely to draw support than elaborate plans. Most successful programs began small and grew incrementally (Ewell, 1988). The assessment efforts at Alverno College and Northeast Missouri State University have been underway for a decade and a half. It should be clear to all concerned, however, that any "pilot" project is not a test of whether the campus will proceed with assessment but of how to do so in the most efficient and effective manner.

An inventory of current data collection activities (including the use of standardized measures, program review results, surveys, and standard institutional research studies) can be a politically and practically useful beginning. All academic and administrative offices should be surveyed to identify the information already on hand about students and about the effectiveness of their unit's activities. Such an inventory is likely to reveal far greater involvement in "assessment" than might at first have been believed.

In sum, one cannot overstate the importance of laying a strong political foundation. Without it, the assessment structure cannot stand. Faculty members, department heads, and deans are keen observers of their administrative superiors and readily discern which attitudes and behaviors are rewarded and which are not. For any assessment program to succeed, there simply must be some payoff for faculty members, whether in the form of additional funding to correct identified program deficiencies, rewards for a job well done (say, some extra travel money), or other incentives to engage in assessment and enhance the quality of teaching and learning in a department.

Coordination. Assessment requires the involvement of a wide variety of people and offices, crossing not only academic departmental lines but vice-presidential areas as well. Alternative approaches to the campus-wide coordination problem include assignment of coordinating responsibility to a currently existing office already significantly engaged in assessment and controlling many of the necessary resources (for example, the office of institutional research), creation of a new office, or assignment to a committee with representatives from the major affected organizational areas (Ewell, 1988). Each of these approaches has its assets and liabilities, of course, and though space precludes a detailed discussion of each, the reporting lines for the office or group should be given careful attention. Whatever approach is adopted, what will be the likely effects on traditional areas of responsibility and lines of authority? On informal power networks? On traditional distinctions between academic and student affairs? Ways will have to be found to coordinate activities in such a way that lines of authority and responsibility are clear, existing functions and activities are not duplicated, and support is received from each area (Ewell, 1988). As noted earlier, experience indicates that the support of the institutions' top executives, particularly the president and chief academic officer, must be active and visible, especially in the early stages of the program's development.

Costs. How much should an institution invest in its assessment program? The answer, of course, will depend on the purposes and the extensiveness of the assessment program and its activities. Ewell and Jones

(1986) have argued that the real question is one of marginal costs: "How much *more* money beyond that already committed to outcomes-related information gathering do we have to spend to put in place an assessment program that is appropriate to our needs?" (p. 34). These costs are incurred in four areas: (1) instruments, (2) administration, (3) analysis, and (4) coordination. Rossmann and El-Khawas (1987) also note start-up costs, which can include consultant services, conference attendance and visits to other campuses, on-campus workshops, and faculty and staff time for organizing and perhaps instrument development.

According to Rossmann and El-Khawas (1987), campuses with ongoing assessment programs spend ten to fifteen dollars per enrolled student. Ewell and Jones (1986), after making a series of assumptions about the nature of the assessment program likely to be mounted by institutions of varying types and sizes, estimate incremental costs ranging from $30,000 (for a small, private, liberal arts college) to $130,000 (for a major public research university). These latter estimates do not include personnel costs associated with faculty involvement in assessment.

Finally, opportunity costs must also be considered. Institutional resources (including time) invested in assessment are not available for investment elsewhere. Moreover, [former] Governor Kean (1987) of New Jersey advised institutions not to ask for additional funds to cover assessment costs. According to Kean, legislators are unlikely to respond favorably to requests for money to determine whether past and current appropriations are being effectively used. If that is true, reallocation of currently appropriated funds will probably be necessary, although a variety of other sources are available, including grants from public agencies, private foundations, individuals, or even student fees to cover testing directly beneficial to students (Rossmann and El-Khawas, 1987).

In considering the costs of assessment, however, the costs of not assessing educational outcomes must also be placed in the balance. Important opportunities may be missed, including, for example, the chance to clarify institutional goals, review and revise (or reconfirm the value of) existing curricular purposes and structures, and examine the successes and failures of current policies and practices. The costs of rejecting or deferring assessment may be substantial, if difficult to calculate.

Methodological Issues

The third major category of potential assessment pitfalls is methodological. Some of these problems are specific to particular approaches to assessment, whereas others are merely common and frequent violations of the canons of good research. Within this general area, potential problems fall into three subcategories: (1) design limitations, (2) measurement difficulties, and (3) statistical hazards.

Design Problems. From the outset, it is important to keep in mind that research design is a series of compromises. Designs that increase the power of a study in one area come almost invariably at the expense of some other aspect of the study. Whenever something is gained, something else is given away. The key to useful and psychometrically sound inquiry is to know what is being gained and what is being given away (see Terenzini, 1980).

The dominant theme in the chorus of demands for "accountability" through assessment is the need to demonstrate that college and university attendance makes a difference, that students leave colleges and universities with knowledge, skills, attitudes, and values they did not have when they arrived. An impressive number of studies (for example, Bowen, 1977; Pace, 1979) demonstrate the fact that students change in a variety of ways between their freshman and senior years. The problem lies in specifying the origins of those changes. Students may change during the college years in response to many influences, including their own precollege characteristics and their noncollege experiences, not to mention normal maturation. Thus, collegiate impact is only one of the possible sources of freshman-to-senior-year change. Collegiate experiences may be a significant source of change, but knowing with any degree of certainty whether and to what extent college has an effect is a very complicated matter.

A common approach to the assessment of change in students is the use of a successive cross-sections design, typically involving cross-sectional samples of current freshmen and senior students. The freshmen (the control group) are compared with the seniors (the treatment group) on some measure of the variables on which change is being studied. Observed differences are then taken as an indication of the effects of the college on students. Such designs have a number of limitations, however, including the need to assume that current seniors, at the time they matriculated, were similar in important respects to current freshmen—a questionable proposition. Such designs also leave selective dropout during the college years uncontrolled. Not all students who begin college will finish it, and students who complete a college program, compared with those who do not, are likely to have higher aptitude and achievement records and greater commitment to college. Given such self-selection during the college years, freshman and senior group score means would probably be different even if the two classes had been identical at the time they entered college. Any changes over the period in admissions standards or recruiting strategies might also have produced initially nonequivalent groups in the two classes.

Pascarella (1987) suggests several ways to reduce the nonequivalent-groups problem inherent in this design. One possibility is to control for age and entering academic aptitude through statistics, matching, or both. Use of samples of freshman and senior students of the same age is another option. Both are preferable, if imperfect, alternatives to the typical, unadjusted, successive cross-sections design.

NEW DIRECTIONS FOR INSTITUTIONAL RESEARCH • DOI: 10.1002/ir

Longitudinal designs are a frequently recommended alternative. One might measure the characteristics of an entering freshman class in a variety of areas and then, after a period of time (for example, two or four years), study the group again and compare students with themselves at the time they entered college, controlling for entering characteristics. At least some of the same people are being studied at the two different times, but the tendency of subjects to drop out of a study over time can be a significant problem with longitudinal research, particularly research that covers an extended period of time (for example, four years). As response rates drop, study generalizability is threatened.

Ideally, one would follow over the same period of time a control group of high school graduates who do not attend college (but who are presumably personally and academically equivalent to one's freshmen) and who could be compared after some period of time with the freshman group who have presumably benefited from college attendance. Although the equivalency of groups might be questioned even under this sampling plan, the design has obvious advantages over a successive cross-sections design. Obtaining a sample of students who do not attend college may be difficult; however, it may be reasonable for institutions serving a largely local or regional population (for example, community and commuting colleges). Institutions that draw students from a national base will probably find this alternative impractical.

The price paid for adopting a longitudinal design comes in several forms. Because of the unavoidable subject mortality problem, longitudinal designs also require larger samples. Increased sample sizes mean higher direct and indirect costs for personnel and materials, as well as more complex data management requirements. Finally, longitudinal studies take longer to complete, and all too often the need for information is (or is thought to be) immediate.

Another group assessment pitfall arises in developing a sampling plan. Have clearly in mind the kinds of subgroup analyses that are planned, for as the number of groups grows or if one or more subgroups come from a small population (for example, minority students), simple random sampling may be inappropriate. Experience indicates, for example, that successful assessment programs provide unit-specific information. It is easy for deans or department heads to disregard assessment information when it comes from students or alumni of other schools or departments. The implication of this advice, however, often overlooked until it is too late, is that a census, not a sample, of students must be taken. Otherwise group sizes may be too small to have face validity, political believability, or statistical stability. Costs and workload will, of course, go up accordingly.

Measurement Problems. However one defines "assessment," it will involve some form of measurement, and sooner or later one must deal with the problems and hazards of instrument selection. The common dilemma is whether to "buy, build, or borrow." Should one adopt a commercially available measure (for example, ACT's COMP or Collegiate Assessment of Academic Proficiency[CAAP], or ETS's Academic Profile)? Or should one devise an instrument locally, or perhaps use a measure developed for similar purposes on some other campus? As noted previously, research is a series of compromises. Nationally available measures have several advantages, the first of which is that they have been developed by experts. Second, they have been field-tested, and their psychometric properties are known. Third, national scores or norms are usually available so one can compare one's students with those of other campuses of similar size, type, and purpose. Finally, use of commercial instruments can save substantial amounts of time and expense that would be required for local instrument development.

Such advantages come at a cost, however. In order to be usable in a variety of settings and for a variety of purposes, commercial measures are necessarily general and lack the specificity needed to focus in any detail on local conditions. Standardized achievement measures also focus unavoidably on a limited number of learning objectives. Do the substantive knowledge and skills measured by those instruments coincide with those that faculty want students to learn? Centra (1987) calls attention to the "faulty assumption . . . that commercial, standardized tests will adequately measure the student learning objectives of a typical general education program. But in fact it is unlikely that any of the tests measure more than half of what most faculty members believe should be part of general education" (p. 2).

Moreover, the format of any given measure constrains the range of what it can assess. For example, many standardized tests employ a multiple-choice structure that, no matter how clearly items may be written, limits the range of aspects of an educational outcome that can be examined (Baird, 1987). One must remember that standardized, machine-scored tests were developed (and are popular) because they are comparatively easy to use, not because they are the best way to measure something. Centra (1987) recommends that if commercial instruments are adopted, they be supplemented with local measures.

On the other hand, though locally developed measures may be more carefully tailored to local purposes and educational objectives, they are also likely to be untested (at least in the short run) and, consequently, of unknown reliability and validity. Moreover, instrument construction is neither inexpensive nor an activity for novices. Many faculty members will have neither the time, commitment, nor competence to develop local measures.

As suggested earlier, the validity of assessments can be increased through the use of multiple measures. The allegory of the blind men seeking to describe the elephant has an important lesson to offer. Psychometricians know that each type of measurement has its characteristic sources of error (Sechrest and Phillips, 1969), and reliance on one measure (or type of measure) is likely to produce data systematically biased by that measure's characteristic sources of error. In adopting multiple measures, one samples their strengths and their weaknesses, and as the number of different measures increases, so does the likelihood that any given measure's weaknesses will be counterbalanced by the strength(s) of another.

One source of error characteristic of many of the assessment measures currently in use (commercially or locally developed) is their reactivity. Respondents to tests and surveys know they are being studied and that knowledge may influence their responses in varying and unknown ways. Such intrusive methods influence and shape, as well as measure. Unobtrusive measures—ones that do not require a conscious response from the subject—can be highly useful as well as efficient. For example, if one wishes to know whether students are receiving a general education, one alternative to the intrusive testing of students is an analysis of their transcripts. How many credits does the typical undergraduate take in various disciplinary areas? When are those credits earned (for example lower- or upper-division years)? How do these course-taking patterns vary across major fields? Transcript analysis is a reasonable basis for inference about the breadth and depth of students' formal learning (Warren, 1984), and numerous other unobtrusive measures are available to creative researchers (Terenzini, 1987).

Even if one successfully avoids these measurement pitfalls, however, additional hazards lie ahead as one begins the analysis of the data those assessment devices produce. The certainty implied by statistical testing can mask problems that may lead to the serious misinterpretation of results.

Statistical Problems. As noted previously, assessment (particularly the accountability strain) has embedded in it the expectation that change will occur, that the institution's contribution to student learning can be made apparent and even measured with some precision. Unfortunately, we rely almost without exception on average changes (for example, a comparison of a group mean at time 1 with the same group's mean at time 2). Group change, however, often masks individual change. Any observed freshman-to-senior-year group change is related to the number of students who change and the amount of change each student experiences. It may be useful to give attention to the frequency, direction, and magnitude of individual changes (Feldman and Newcomb, 1969).

Moreover, change is often construed as "value-added," a frequently heard phrase that can be highly misleading and damaging if not understood. Warren (1984) and Pascarella (1987) offer thoughtful and detailed discussions of this concept, but certain aspects of it require attention here. "Value-added" is both a metaphor and a research design. As a metaphor, it is a vivid and useful term focusing our attention on institutional effects rather than resources. Unfortunately, it can sometimes be too vivid, leading people inside and outside the academy to expect more of our assessment programs than can possibly be delivered. The reason for this lies not only in the metaphor's implication that "change" occurs, but also that it is positive change or growth. Can "value" be "added" without positive change? Legislators and others are likely to say no. And therein lies the perniciousness of the metaphor, for it is important to distinguish "change" from collegiate "impact." As Pascarella (1987) notes: "In some areas of development . . . the impact of college (or other educational experiences) may be to prevent or retard decline rather than to induce major positive changes. Consequently, approaches to value-added assessment which focus only on pre- to post-changes may be overlooking important college effects" (p. 78). For example, Wolfle (1983) found that mathematics performance among a national sample of high school graduates declined over the seven years following graduation. The data suggest, however, that the effects of college attendance may be to maintain precollege mathematics performance levels, whereas math achievement declines among those who do not go to college.

Similarly, it will be well to remember that one variable (for example, some aspect of the college experience) can influence another variable (for example, some outcome measure) in both direct and indirect ways. For example, evidence indicates that whereas participation in a prematriculation orientation program has no direct influence on freshman persistence into the sophomore year, attendance at an orientation session does positively influence students' level of social integration, which, in turn, is positively related to sophomore year enrollment (Pascarella, Terenzini, and Wolfle, 1986). Thus, any "value-added" approach that fails to take into account the indirect, as well as the direct, effects of college is likely to underestimate the full range of the collegiate influence (Pace, 1979).

One must also remember that college effects may not manifest themselves right way. For example, it is probably unreasonable to expect significant student progress over a one- or two-year period in acquiring the intellectual and personal knowledge, skills, attitudes, and values presumed to characterize a liberal education. Faculty, administrators, students, parents, and legislators must not expect (or be led to expect) more of assessment programs than can reasonably be delivered. The benefits college is supposed to impart are not acquired overnight, and the programs intended to assess these benefits take time to design, implement, and fine-tune.

The "value-added" metaphor also promotes an analytical design that is correspondingly simple but potentially more dangerous. Common sense suggests that if one wishes to know whether something changes over time, one should measure it at time 1 and again at time 2. The difference between the pre- and posttest scores—the "change" score—presumably reflects the effects of some process. To many, this change score reflects the institutional "value added." In this instance, however, common sense may harm more than help. Indeed, change scores have some positively alarming characteristics.

For example, simple difference scores are highly unreliable, and they can be shown to be negatively correlated with pretest scores (Linn and Slinde, 1977). Second, it can also be shown that the higher the correlation between pre- and posttest measures, the lower the reliability of the gain score (Linn and Slinde, 1977). Such unreliability makes detection of reliable associations with other variables (for example, aspects of the institutional experience thought to produce a portion of the change) more difficult.

Third, simple difference scores are also subject to ceiling effects: students with high pretest scores have little room for improvement and thus are likely to show smaller gains than students with lower initial scores. Similarly, gain scores are subject to regression effects, the tendency—due strictly to measurement error—for initially high (or low) scores to move ("regress") toward the group mean upon subsequent retesting.

One or more of these reasons probably lies behind the results reported by Banta et al. (1987). Many institutions are unable or unwilling to wait the usual two to four years needed for a longitudinal study following a cohort of entering freshmen through to the completion of a degree program. For that reason, and using the correlation between students' senior-year College Outcomes Measures Project (COMP) scores and their freshman year ACT Assessment Composite scores, the ACT has constructed concordance tables that permit institutions to estimate the COMP score gain, or value-added, that might have been recorded if the students had taken the COMP test in both freshman and senior years (Banta et al., 1987).

In a series of tests on these estimated gain scores, Banta et al. (1987) made a number of striking (if not to say bizarre) findings. They found, for example, that the estimated gains for University of Tennessee-Knoxville students were underestimated by as much as 60 percent. Moreover, a large number of seniors had no ACT Assessment Composite score from which to estimate a gain score, and the students without assessment scores tended to be older, black, and from lower socioeconomic families, raising serious questions about the generalizability of any study based on estimated gain scores. Finally, the correlations between estimated gain scores and certain demographic and institutional variables were the opposite of what was expected. For example, the greatest gain scores tended to be those of students who had high school averages lower than 3.0, did not receive a scholarship, whose fathers did not graduate from college, who did not participate in honors mathematics sections, and who did not take more than two mathematics courses (Banta et al., 1987). In all likelihood, these startling findings are due to the unreliability of gain scores, as well as to ceiling and regression effects.

Such results raise serious questions about the reliability and validity of any estimated gain score, not just those produced using the ACT's COMP and assessment instruments. Indeed, Banta and her colleagues (1987) are quick to praise COMP as a "valuable tool for stimulating faculty discussion about the general education curriculum, and modes of instructions. . . . What is called into question is the usefulness, the validity, of employing *estimated* student score gain on the COMP for the purpose of making precise judgments about program quality that can serve as the basis for decisions about the allocation of resources in higher education" (p. 19). And though one might infer from this that the use of actual gain scores may be a way of circumventing the problems Banta and her colleagues identified, the same problems afflict actual gain scores as well.

Thus, in considering the use of the "value-added" metaphor in a specific measurement setting, one would be well advised to follow the suggestion of Cronbach and Furby (1970), who advised "investigators who ask questions regarding gain scores [to] frame their questions in other ways" (p. 80). Centra (1987) recommends "a criterion-referenced approach in which the level and content of student learning is compared to standards and objectives established by the faculty and staff of a college" (p. 8). A variant on that approach is to examine the trend over time in the proportion of students who score above a faculty-determined threshold of "acceptable" performance on any given measure. Linn and Slinde (1977) and Pascarella (1987) suggest a number of other alternatives, although space precludes their review here. The point is that there are conceptually understandable and methodologically preferable alternatives to the use of simple difference scores.

Finally, whether one is dealing with design, measurement, or analytical issues, it will be well to remember that campus-based assessment programs are intended to gather information for instructional, programmatic, and institutional improvement, not for journal publication. Methodological standards for research publishable in scholarly and professional journals can probably be relaxed in the interests of institutional utility and advancement. The most appropriate test of the suitability of a design, measure, or analytical procedure is probably that of reasonableness (Pascarella, 1987): Was the study conducted with reasonable fidelity to the canons of sound research? Given the constraints on the research methods used and the data produced, is it reasonable to infer that college has had an effect on student change? Although the methodological issues reviewed here cannot and should not be ignored, neither should one's concern about them stifle action.

Conclusion

The assessment of student outcomes has much to offer colleges and universities. In linking stated institutional and programmatic goals to the measurement of progress toward their achievement, assessment represents a significant refocusing of institutional efforts on the purposes and effectiveness of undergraduate education. Assessment requires consideration of three questions: (1) What should a student get out of college? (2) What should a student get out of attending this college? and (3) What does a student get from attending this college? Addressing these questions in a systematic, periodic assessment program is likely to foster increased clarity about the purposes of an undergraduate program (one can also engage in assessment at the graduate level), increased consensus on those goals, and a better understanding of the consequences of educational policies and programs. In many respects, assessment is really only something higher education should have been doing all along.

The assessment of student outcomes, however, is not something that can be done quickly or casually. Several conceptual, administrative, political, and methodological issues may prove troublesome in developing a successful and beneficial assessment program. At the same time, and with a little preparation and care, those pitfalls can be rather easily avoided. This chapter has sought to help in those preparations by increasing the likelihood that when a campus starts down the path to assessment, it will do so with open eyes.

References

Astin, A. W. *Achieving Educational Excellence*. San Francisco: Jossey-Bass, 1985.

Baird, L. L. "Diverse and Subtle Arts: Assessing the Generic Academic Outcomes of Higher Education." Paper presented to the Association for the Study of Higher Education, Baltimore, 1987.

Banta, T, W., Lambert, E., Pike, G., Schmidhammer, J., and Schneider, J. "Estimated Student Score Gain on the ACT COMP Exam: Valid Tool for Institutional Assessment?" *Research in Higher Education*, 1987, 27, 195–217.

Bloom, B. S., Englehart, M., Furst, E., Hill, W., and Krathwohl, D. *Taxonomy of Educational Objectives: Handbook I. Cognitive Domain*. New York: McKay, 1956.

Bowen, H. R. *Investment in Learning: The Individual and Social Value of American Higher Education*. San Francisco: Jossey-Bass, 1977.

Centra, J. A. "Assessing the Content Areas of General Education." Paper presented to the Association for the Study of Higher Education, Baltimore, 1987.

Cronbach, L. J., and. Furby, L. "How We Should Measure 'Change'—or Should We?" *Psychological Bulletin*, 1970, 74, 68–80.

Ewell, P. T. *The Self-Regarding Institution: Information for Excellence*. Boulder, CO: National Center for Higher Education Management Systems, 1984.

Ewell, P. T. "Assessment: Where Are We?" *Change*, 1987a, 19, 23–28.

Ewell, P. T. "Establishing a Campus-Based Assessment Program." In D. F. Halpern (ed.), *Student Outcomes Assessment: What Institutions Stand to Gain*. New Directions for Higher Education, no. 59. San Francisco: Jossey-Bass, 1987b.

Ewell, P. T. "Implementing Assessment: Some Organizational Issues." In T. W. Banta and H. S. Fisher (eds.), *Implementing Outcomes Assessment: Promise and Perils*. New Directions for Institutional Research, no. 59. San Francisco: Jossey-Bass, 1988.

Ewell, P. T., and Jones, D. "The Costs of Assessment." In C. Adelman (ed.), *Assessment in American Higher Education: Issues and Contexts*. Washington, DC: U.S. Office of Education, Office of Educational Research and Improvement, 1986.

Feldman, K. A., and Newcomb, T. M. *The Impact of College on Students*. San Francisco: Jossey-Bass, 1969.

Kean, T. H. "Time to Deliver Before We Forget the Promises We Made." *Change*, Sept./Oct. 1987, 19, 10–11.

Krathwohl, D. R., Bloom, B. S., and Masia, B. B. *Taxonomy of Educational Objectives: The Classification of Educational Goals. Handbook II: Affective Domain*. New York: McKay, 1964.

Lenning, O. T. *The Outcomes Structure: An Overview and Procedure for Applying It in Postsecondary Education Institutions*. Boulder, CO: National Center for Higher Education Management Systems, 1979.

Linn, R. L., and Slinde, J. A. "The Determination of the Significance of Change Between Pre- and Posttesting Periods." *Review of Educational Research*, 1977, 47, 121–150.

Northeast Missouri State University. *In Pursuit of Degrees with Integrity: A Value Added Approach to Undergraduate Assessment*. Washington, DC: American Association of State Colleges and Universities, 1984.

Pace, C. R. *Measuring the Outcomes of College: Fifty Years of Findings and Recommendations for the Future.* San Francisco: Jossey-Bass, 1979.

Pascarella, E. T. "Are Value-Added Analyses Valuable?" In *Assessing the Outcomes of Higher Education.* Proceedings of the 1986 ETS Invitational Conference, Princeton, NJ: Educational Testing Service, 1987.

Pascarella, E. T., Terenzini, P. T., and Wolfle, L. M. "Orientation to College and Freshman Year Persistence/Withdrawal Decisions." *Journal of Higher Education,* 1986, *57,* 155–175.

Rossmann, J. E., and El-Khawas, E. *Thinking About Assessment: Perspectives for Presidents and Chief Academic Officers.* Washington, DC: American Council on Education, 1987.

Sechrest, L., and Phillips, M. "Unobtrusive Measures: An Overview." In L. Sechrest (ed.), *Unobtrusive Measurement Today.* New Directions for Methodology of Behavioral Science, no. 1. San Francisco: Jossey-Bass, 1969.

Terenzini, P. T. "An Evaluation of Three Basic Designs for Studying Attrition." *Journal of College Student Personnel, 21,* 1980, 257–263.

Terenzini, P. T. "The Case for Unobtrusive Measures." In *Assessing the Outcomes of Higher Education.* Princeton, NJ: Educational Testing Service, 1987. (ED 284895)

Warren, J. "The Blind Alley of Value Added." *AAHE Bulletin,* 1984, *37,* 10–13.

Wolfle, L. M. "Effects of Higher Education on Ability for Blacks and Whites." *Research in Higher Education,* 1983, *19,* 3–10.

Yanikoski, R. A. Comments made as part of a panel discussion on Measuring the Value of College. Annual Meeting of the Illinois Association for Institutional Research, Champaign, Nov. 1987.

PATRICK T. TERENZINI *is Distinguished Professor of Higher Education and Senior Scientist in the Center for the Study of Higher Education at The Pennsylvania State University.*

NEW DIRECTIONS FOR INSTITUTIONAL RESEARCH • DOI: 10.1002/ir

4

The chapter offers four practical suggestions for implementing campus assessment programs based on an accreditation self-study at a research university.

Overcoming Obstacles to Campus Assessment

J. Fredericks Volkwein

Despite their apparent popularity among those seeking degrees and credentials, today's colleges and universities face several interrelated public criticisms and concerns. First, many students are not successful, and few campuses can explain why. Some students are highly successful, others struggle and take longer to graduate, and still other students seem to disappear after a semester or two. A second related concern regards organizational productivity and inefficiency. Virtually every sector of the economy except education has made substantial gains in productivity over the years. Considerable resources are devoted to the processes of recruiting, educating, and graduating diverse populations of students in a competitive environment. Student dropouts and delays in college completion draw attention to costly inefficiencies in the educational system. A third related concern, expressed by parents, college students, and taxpayers alike, pertains to the high cost of higher education. Since 1970, tuition and fees on public and private campuses alike have risen on average at a rate that is double the increases in the Consumer Price Index. The fourth concern focuses on educational effectiveness. Most customers are willing to pay more for higher quality and better service, but it is not clear that higher tuition prices translate into higher quality. There is ample evidence from employers and researchers alike that many college graduates are not as well educated, or as employable, as they were in the past and as they need to be in the future.

When these competing concerns about student success, productivity, cost, and educational effectiveness all collide at the campus level, they

NEW DIRECTIONS FOR INSTITUTIONAL RESEARCH, Assessment Supplement 2009, Spring 2010 © Wiley Periodicals, Inc.
Published online in Wiley InterScience (www.interscience.wiley.com) • DOI: 10.1002/ir.330

create an array of campus tensions for campus leaders, planners, institutional researchers, and student affairs administrators at all levels (Volkwein, 1999). This chapter describes how universities can use, and have used, systems of local data gathering to respond to these concerns with facts and evidence to better inform internal and external stakeholders, as well as to take corrective action.

In Chapter Three, Terenzini identified a number of assessment pitfalls and offered constructive suggestions for overcoming them. This chapter extends that discussion with four practical steps that can be taken locally by the campus to alleviate these concerns: avoid the paralysis of the grand plan, start with an outcomes model or conceptual framework, conduct an inventory of existing information, and use the results for constructive organizational change.

Avoid the Paralysis of the Grand Plan

Although assessment plans are beneficial organizers and guides for data collection and analysis, campuses should avoid the paralysis of the grand plan: an attitude, typical in academic organizations, that there must be a comprehensive, long-range research plan for data collection and analysis and that nothing can be done until there is administrative, faculty, and governance agreement. In the real world outside academe, successful research and analysis often starts simply with existing evaluative efforts and data and then builds on them. Rather than the scholarly strategy of starting with a research question and then designing a scientifically controlled data collection, it is often advantageous to work backward from existing data sources and examine what questions can be answered from them before collecting new data. Getting started in this way can produce early findings that not only influence campus decisions and policy but also enhance subsequent, more formal data collection.

Start with an Outcomes Model or Conceptual Framework

Whether derived from the research literature, adapted from another college, or developed locally, an outcomes model encourages clarity of thought, serves as an organizer for both existing and new data collection and analysis, and makes campus assessment efforts more efficient. A model-driven system of periodic data collection also avoids the expensive trap, sometimes stimulated by accountability pressures, of believing that you need to measure everything all the time.

Higher education scholarship has produced an array of theories and models that explain the relationship between students and their colleges. Drawing from this pool of available models, at least four major assertions regarding the interactions between students and their colleges, and the

NEW DIRECTIONS FOR INSTITUTIONAL RESEARCH • DOI: 10.1002/ir

influences of collegiate experiences on student outcomes can be cited. The most traditional view is that precollege characteristics such as student backgrounds, academic preparedness for college, and clear goals are the main factors accounting for differences in academic performance, persistence behavior, and other educational outcomes (Astin, 1991; Feldman and Newcomb, 1969; Stark, Shaw, and Lowther, 1989).

A second group of perspectives falls under the general description of student-institution fit models. Perhaps the most widely researched of these models claims that student persistence and growth depend on the degree of successful integration into the academic and social structures of the institution (Spady, 1970, 1971; Tinto, 1987, 1993). Other student-institution fit models focus on the importance of student involvement and effort (Astin, 1984; Pace, 1984; Kuh, Pace, and Vesper, 1997), the importance of support from friends and family in college adjustment (Bean, 1980; Bean and Metzner, 1985; Cabrera, Castaneda, Nora, and Hengstler, 1992; Nora, 1987), and financial variables and the student's ability to pay (Cabrera, Stampen, and Hansen, 1990; Cabrera, Nora, and Castenada, 1993a, 1993b; St. John, 1992). While the majority of these models have been constructed to explain one outcome, student persistence, several researchers have successfully used these and similar other models to explain other outcomes, including student growth and satisfaction (Terenzini, Pascarella, and Lorang, 1982; Terenzini, Theophilides, and Lorang, 1984a, 1984b; Terenzini and Wright, 1987a, 1987b; Terenzini, Springer, Pascarella, and Nora, 1995; Volkwein, King, and Terenzini, 1986; Volkwein, 1991; Volkwein and Lorang, 1996; Volkwein, Valle, Blose, and Zhou, 2000; Strauss and Volkwein, 2002). One model has been presented to explain the educational outcomes of community college students (Voorhees, 1997). More than others, the Voorhees model emphasizes the competing demands of family, work, and community.

A third set of assertions emphasizes the importance of campus climate in student adjustment (Bauer, 1998). Perceptions of prejudice, discrimination, racial harmony, and tolerance of diversity have gained increased attention as factors accounting for the differences in persistence rates between minorities and nonminorities (Cabrera, Nora, Terenzini, Pascarella, and Hagedorn, 1999; Fleming, 1984; Hurtado, 1992, 1994; Hurtado, Carter, and Spuler, 1996; Loo and Rolison, 1986; Nora and Cabrera, 1996; Smedley, Myers, and Harrell, 1993). All students need to be able to function in a safe environment, without fear of oppression, stigma, and violence, in order to maximize their chances of success (Reynolds, 1999). Creating a campus climate for all students that allows optimal development is a major factor in successful student outcomes (Upcraft and Schuh, 1996).

Fourth, structural perspectives, drawing from the literature on organizations, encourage researchers to give greater attention to variables that reflect the influence of organizational characteristics (Hall 1992; Volkwein and Szelest, 1995; Strauss and Volkwein, 2002). Studies of colleges and universities, as particular types of organizations, have shown that campus mission, size, expenditures, complexity, and selectivity exert small but significant influences on a variety of internal transactions and outcomes, including student learning and skills, values, aspirations, and educational and career attainment (Pascarella and Terenzini, 1991; Volkwein, Szelest, Cabrera, and Napierski-Prancl, 1998; Toutkoushian and Smart, 2001). In their synthesis of the literature, Berger and Milem (2000) conclude that an array of organizational features and behaviors influences student experiences and outcomes. The Berger and Milem conceptual model extends the Pascarella model (1985) and the Weidman model (1989). These are the earliest models that give prominence to campus organizational behaviors and structural characteristics as influences on student outcomes.

These four perspectives—precollege characteristics, student-institution fit, campus climate, and organizational characteristics—provide complementary theories regarding the influences on educational outcomes. In order to capture a holistic perspective of educational outcomes and to respond sensibly to campus environmental problems, it is useful to start with a model to guide the development of measures and data collection. The most straightforward approach is to start with a simple input-process-output (IPO) model. Two such models are shown here, and they have served as organizers for research conducted at Penn State University and the State University of New York at Albany. Both models (displayed in Figures 4.1 and 4.2) assume that a variety of outcomes (outputs) are the products first of characteristics and experiences that students bring with them (inputs), and second of their various college experiences inside and outside the classroom (processes).

The model originally developed by Patrick Terenzini for the National Study of Student Learning at Penn State (the Terenzini-Reason Comprehensive Outcomes Model) has been enhanced over the years and serves as a good organizer for gathering categories of information related to learning outcomes. Figure 4.1 shows the latest version of the Terenzini-Reason model. The Albany Outcomes Model, developed by Volkwein (1991, 1992, 2003), suggests in greater detail some of the information items and scales that reflect the four perspectives and concepts from the literature discussed above. The educational outcomes in the Albany model are products of a multiyear strategic planning and mission development process that identified particular goals and outcomes for undergraduate education at the institution. Each outcome can be examined in relation to the precollege and college experiences that produced it.

Conduct an Inventory of Existing Information

Many campus offices store information that is potentially useful once it is examined for its relevance to an effectiveness model or to mission goal attainment. Academic departments and administrative offices alike

Figure 4.1. Terenzini-Reason Comprehensive Outcomes Model

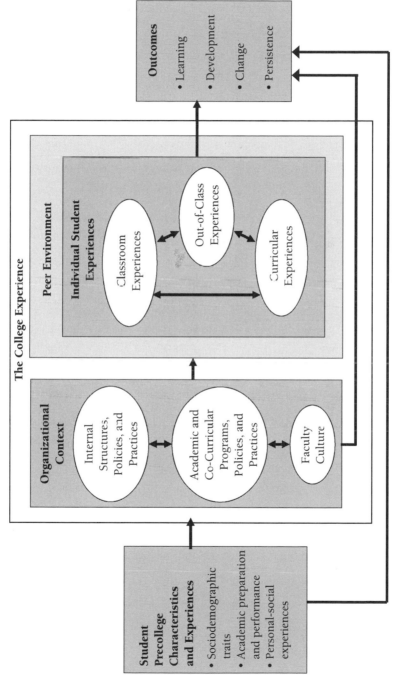

Sources: Terenzini and Reason (2005); Reason, Terenzini, and Domingo (2006).

Figure 4.2. Albany Outcomes Model

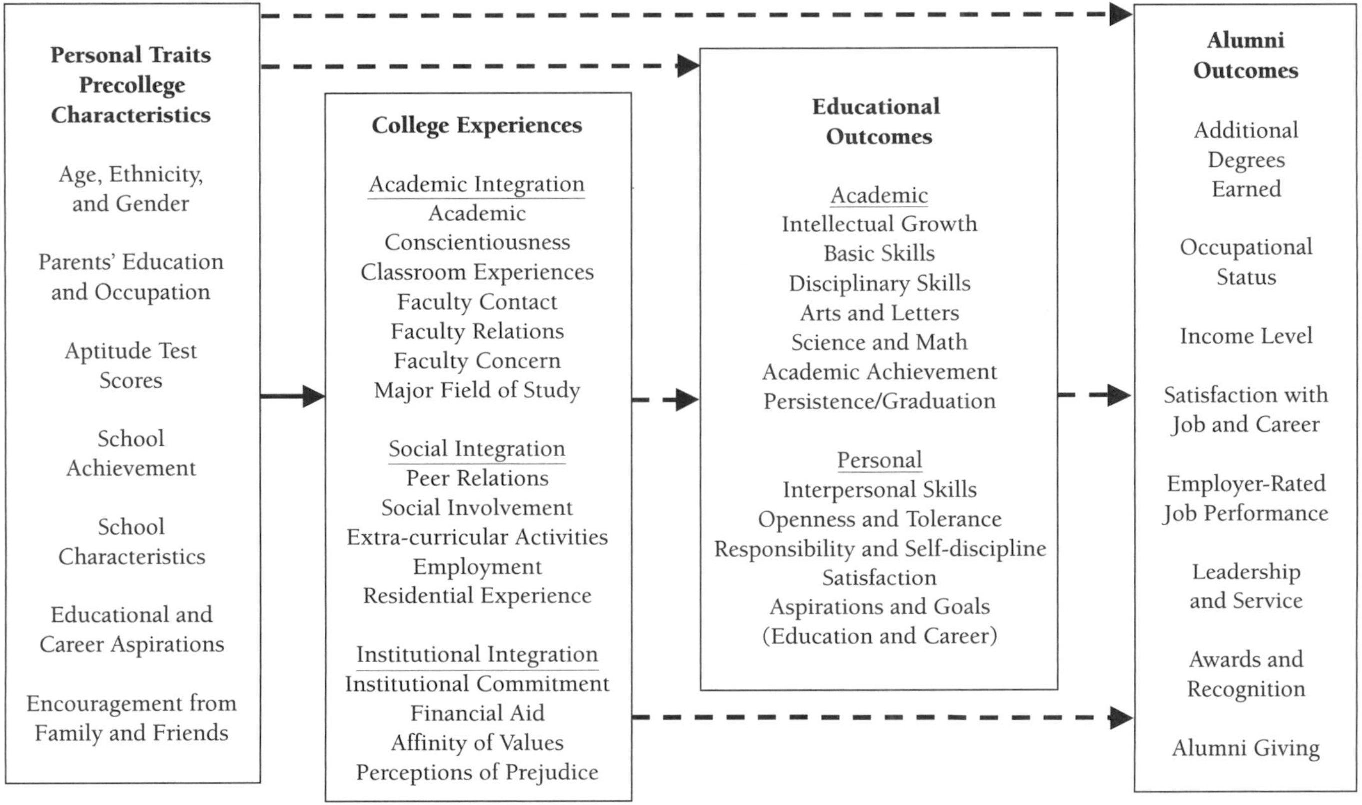

Personal Traits Precollege Characteristics

Age, Ethnicity, and Gender

Parents' Education and Occupation

Aptitude Test Scores

School Achievement

School Characteristics

Educational and Career Aspirations

Encouragement from Family and Friends

College Experiences

Academic Integration
Academic Conscientiousness
Classroom Experiences
Faculty Contact
Faculty Relations
Faculty Concern
Major Field of Study

Social Integration
Peer Relations
Social Involvement
Extra-curricular Activities
Employment
Residential Experience

Institutional Integration
Institutional Commitment
Financial Aid
Affinity of Values
Perceptions of Prejudice

Educational Outcomes

Academic
Intellectual Growth
Basic Skills
Disciplinary Skills
Arts and Letters
Science and Math
Academic Achievement
Persistence/Graduation

Personal
Interpersonal Skills
Openness and Tolerance
Responsibility and Self-discipline
Satisfaction
Aspirations and Goals (Education and Career)

Alumni Outcomes

Additional Degrees Earned

Occupational Status

Income Level

Satisfaction with Job and Career

Employer-Rated Job Performance

Leadership and Service

Awards and Recognition

Alumni Giving

Source: http://www.Albany.edu/ir/reports.html.

sometimes collect information that they lack the time and resources to examine thoroughly. Offices engaged in student advisement and services and support activities frequently survey students and collect information that has value beyond the particular operation. Campuses should launch new data collection activities only after reviewing and learning from what is already available. Sources of information can include:

- Admissions and student recruitment data
- Surveys of prospective and entering students
- Financial need and aid data
- Student ratings of instruction
- Retention and graduation rates for different student subgroups
- Frequency of use data for services and facilities
- Academic program reviews
- Reviews and evaluations of offices, services, and facilities
- Academic testing and course placement exams
- Surveys by various offices of particular student or faculty populations
- Career placement, alumni reunion, and alumni survey information
- Exit interview and survey information from departing students and faculty
- Student transcript request data
- Fundraising data
- Student transcripts with enrollments and grades in courses and majors, academic standing, and credits earned elsewhere

This inventory can be a particularly useful exercise if it is taken to the next step: matching the data and information against an outcomes model. Table 4.1 illustrates how this looked at a particular university. Arraying the data in this way sets the stage for analytical studies that examine the connections among all these variables.

Use the Results for Constructive Organizational Change

The balance of this chapter describes the way one campus used local data to address important policy problems and shape decisions. The example begins with a set of local data that reflects an array of measures about student precollege characteristics, college experiences, and outcomes. Every campus has a strategic self-interest in periodically collecting such data and maintaining such data sets. The example described is entirely transportable to other campuses. This university used an accreditation self-study as a stimulus to aggregate the results from several multivariate outcomes studies. This exercise draws a powerful conclusion about the impact the university is having on its students and what matters most.

NEW DIRECTIONS FOR INSTITUTIONAL RESEARCH • DOI: 10.1002/ir

Table 4.1. Classification of Local Variables into Categories That Are Consistent With the Albany Model

Precollege Variables:	Total SAT score	High school average
	Ethnicity/diversity	Class rank
	Male/female	Graduate school aspirations
	Age	Science and math oriented
	Financial need	Goals for major and career
	Parent's education	Service/activities/leadership
	Special abilities/interests—Athletics, art, music, theatre Entry status, transfer credit, advanced placement, marital status, and dependent children	
College Experiences:		
Academic Integration:	Classroom experiences	Faculty relations/advisement
	Study habits	Faculty contact-social
	Remediation	Faculty contact-academic
Social Integration:	Peer relations	Social/activities involvement
	Perceptions of climate	Hours employed on/off-
	Financial aid mix	campus
	Use of, and satisfaction with, services/facilities	Support from friends/family
Outcomes:	Cumulative GPA	Would attend "all over again"
	Goal clarity	Additional degree aspirations
	Retention/graduation	Loan repayment/default
	Time to degree	Overall satisfaction
Intellectual Growth in:	General education skills	Social and behavioral sciences
	Arts, letters, & humanities	Science and engineering
Personal Growth in:	Interpersonal skills	Responsibility/self-control
	Openness/tolerance	Leadership/team building

Colleges and universities undergo regular scrutiny by both regional and specialized accrediting bodies. Historically the purpose of accreditation has been summative, for quality assurance. However, campus officials strain at the workload associated with multiple self-studies and accreditation visits, and sometimes they see few visible benefits. Administrators and faculty alike dread upcoming reaccreditation reviews because of the human resources and other costs of the self-study process.

The university president in this example wanted to use the upcoming regional reaccreditation process to build on and learn from the assessment and evaluation resources of the campus rather than to invest the institution's energy and resources in a one-time process that would evaporate as soon as the site visit team left the campus. In this case, the university prepared for the accreditation self-study by conducting a meta-analysis of all available campus assessment information. The results of this exercise stimulated a host of changes in undergraduate education and in some respects served as a catalyst for organizational transformation.

NEW DIRECTIONS FOR INSTITUTIONAL RESEARCH • DOI: 10.1002/ir

After discussions with the provost and the regional accreditation staff, the president appointed the self-study steering committee and charged it with the task of assembling and summarizing all the assessment and evaluation information on the campus. The offices of academic affairs, student affairs, and institutional research were asked to cooperate with the chair of the steering committee since each of these offices housed analytical expertise. Student affairs periodically collected survey data from entering students as well as campus climate and satisfaction surveys, especially from students in the residence halls. Academic affairs regularly monitored and analyzed student admissions, enrollment, retention, and academic performance statistics, as well as academic program reviews. The office of institutional research was responsible for conducting outcomes studies every three to four years, as well as responding annually to guidebook requests for summary data about students and faculty. Analysts from each of these three offices formed a working group to assemble and integrate the information from these separate sources.

After conducting an inventory of relevant information and studies, the group used an IPO model to classify existing campus data along the lines suggested in the inventory lists shown in Table 4.1. In an exercise that lasted almost a year, the group both summarized the results of existing studies and undertook the analysis of data that had been collected but not systematically studied. Each of the three offices had collected and stored student-level data that had never been linked to existing data in the other offices. The self-study provided the stimulus to examine more thoroughly than before the linkages among precollege characteristics, campus experiences, and subsequent student outcomes.

Figure 4.3 shows some of the results from this collective effort. Each bar in the figure represents the explained variance from one of the multivariate outcomes studies. These studies ranged from analyses of overall satisfaction and cumulative grade point average (GPA), to freshman commitment to attend the university "all over again," to examining self-reported intellectual and personal growth among graduating seniors. The most surprising finding from the figure for the steering committee was the large influence of college experiences for most outcomes and the relatively smaller influence of student precollege traits. Except for cumulative GPA (where SAT scores and high school grades are the best predictors), outcomes were determined the most by what happened to students after they arrived on campus. This was welcome news for the faculty and student affairs staff alike.

The group's next step was to determine the best predictors of each outcome. One group of studies examined the predictors of student academic performance (cumulative GPA) over a ten-year period. In six different studies, student SAT scores, either by themselves or in combination with high school GPA or class rank, were the best predictors of university cumulative GPA. The second most important predictor was self-reported student effort and conscientiousness. A frequently appearing negative influence on

Figure 4.3. Outcomes Measures for University Undergraduates

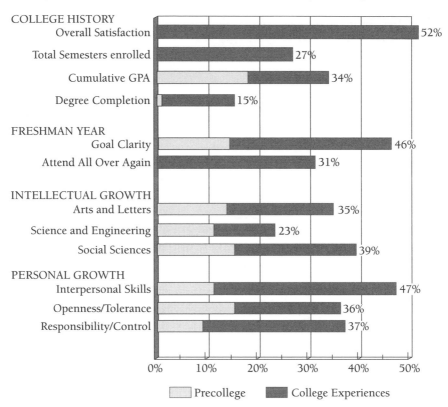

Note: The figure shows the percentage of variance explained by various measures of precollege characteristics and college experiences in multiple studies.

academic performance was working off-campus, especially for twenty or more hours per week.

Analysis of the other outcomes painted a consistent picture of what matters most: classroom experiences, followed by peer relations, faculty relations, and student effort. Classroom experiences were the most powerful contributors to various measures of student outcomes in twenty-one of thirty-three studies at the university over the years. The classroom scale was a set of items developed at the university to reflect the vitality and quality of instruction, stimulating assignments that promote learning, and faculty preparation for class. Classroom vitality was the best predictor of intellectual growth in ten of eleven studies, and in the eleventh, it was a significant secondary contributor. The vitality of the classroom experience was also the most important influence in one study of openness and tolerance, in one study of responsibility and self-control, in two studies of overall satisfaction, in four studies of freshman goal clarity, in two studies of student commitment, and in one study of the length of enrollment.

Peer relations, a scale of items reflecting mostly the strength of student friendships, was the most powerful contributor in one study of openness and tolerance, two studies of interpersonal skill, one study of responsibility and self-control, four studies of student commitment among freshmen, and three studies of student commitment among seniors. Peer relations were strong secondary contributors in several of the other outcomes analyses.

These results are consistent with the literature on student-institution fit. Measures of academic integration, especially classroom experiences, exerted the strongest influences on student growth and satisfaction. Classroom experiences were approximately twice as strong as peer relations and three times stronger than any other significant variables. In nearly all of these studies, few student precollege characteristics proved to be significant. In nine of thirty-three analyses at this campus, small amounts of the variance were explained by financial need, ethnic diversity, and being female. Most other traits that students brought with them consistently failed to achieve significance.

The results of this research synthesis, which continued beyond the period of self-study and reaccreditation, had a far-reaching impact on the campus. Armed with such convincing evidence, the accreditation steering committee made several recommendations in the self-study that were quickly implemented. The convincing evidence about what matters most touched off a series of ongoing discussions ranging from the president's and provost's regular meetings with vice presidents, deans, directors, and chairs to the university senate and its committees. Over the next few years, several changes were implemented:

Greater faculty interest in student learning and growth. In the previous two decades, faculty had been bombarded with information and views suggesting that what happened to students outside the classroom was at least as important as what happened inside it. The self-study brought the faculty role back into prominence and generated greater faculty interest and participation in undergraduate affairs. Knowing the importance of the classroom experience gave faculty greater confidence and pride in their role in undergraduate education at the university.

Alterations in orientation for new students. Prior to these findings, the orientation program for new students was almost entirely a social experience aimed at getting students into clubs, activities, and residential life. The student affairs and academic affairs staffs worked with the faculty to restructure orientation so that the academic component dominated and was aimed at getting students off to a good start academically.

New Directions for Institutional Research • DOI: 10.1002/ir

New academic support services for students. One of the studies of student attrition and academic probation found that a small number of undergraduate courses was responsible for the vast majority of failing grades among freshmen. (Students called them killer courses.) Working with the undergraduate council and the advisement center, the provost and student affairs vice president gave greater attention to academic adjustment and advisement, including the establishment of a peer mentoring program, study skills workshops in the residence halls, and an academic early warning system in killer courses that was linked to tutoring programs.

Residential living-learning communities established with faculty in residence. The provost and student affairs vice president began a series of feasibility studies aimed at creating classrooms and faculty apartments in selected residence hall complexes. In each residential unit, the freshmen take at least one general education course together. The impact of these communities is being evaluated.

Enhanced administrative decision making and strategic planning. The president announced new planning and resource allocation criteria for the campus, which gave top priority to the protection of academic and instructional resources.

Greater attention to faculty development. The provost allocated new resources for an instructional development center to work with faculty on their teaching skills and use of technology.

Centralized institutional research. Instead of institutional analysis being decentralized and spread among the vice-presidential areas, the president's executive team realized the benefits of a centralized office with coordinated data collection and analysis. Thus, the institutional research (IR) analysts in the separate vice-presidential offices were brought together under one director. It was decided that IR constitutes a strategically better, more balanced, and less narrow resource for the institution when the IR team reports to the president's office, but also directs its analytical service to the needs and priorities of the vice presidents. The centralized IR model is more efficient and effective because it takes advantage of the natural economies of scale associated with assessment research expertise, cross-training, and methodological diversity. Also, a centralized arrangement protects the institution better against staff turnover and the inefficiency of narrow specialization. The need for a person to be dedicated to a particular function or task (for example, enrollment management, student climate research, budget analysis, or instructional analysis) can be incorporated into a centralized office and, in fact, better support it, because of the additional expertise and backup that comes with cross-training.

Thus, as a direct consequence of the self-study, the university now had visible outcomes information to support campus planning and decision making, measure attainment of campus and program goals, and demonstrate institutional effectiveness for accreditation. The model-driven process of inventorying and analyzing existing campus data proved to be an effective strategy that supported constructive changes in undergraduate education at the university.

Conclusion

This chapter describes how a campus assembled and analyzed existing data to prepare for reaccreditation and guide constructive academic and administrative improvements. The example demonstrates the value of starting with an outcomes model as an organizing framework both to compile an inventory of existing campus outcomes evidence and analyze that information without waiting to forge a formal assessment plan. Getting started in this way provides an important foundation for a thoughtful and systematic long-range assessment plan.

References

Astin, A. W. *Assessment for excellence: The philosophy and practice of assessment and evaluation in higher education.* New York: MacMillan, 1991.

Astin, A. W. "Student Involvement: A Developmental Theory for Higher Education." *Journal of College Student Personnel*, 1984, 25(4), 297–308.

Bauer, K. W. (ed.). *Campus Climate: Understanding the Critical Components of Today's Colleges and Universities.* New Directions for Institutional Research, no. 98. San Francisco: Jossey-Bass, 1998.

Bean, J. P. "Dropout and Turnover: The Synthesis and Test of a Causal Model of Student Attrition." *Research in Higher Education*, 1980, 12, 155–187.

Bean, J. P., and Metzner, B. S. "A Conceptual Model of Nontraditional Undergraduate Student Attrition." *Review of Higher Educational Research*, 1985, 55(4), 485–540.

Berger, J. B., and Milem, J. F. "Organizational Behavior in Higher Education and Student Outcomes." In J. C. Smart (ed.), *Higher Education Handbook of Theory and Research.* (Vol. 15). New York: Agathon Press, 2000.

Cabrera, A. F., Castaneda, M. B., Nora, A., and Hengstler, D. "The Convergence Between Two Theories of College Persistence." *Journal of Higher Education*, 63(2), 1992, 143–164.

Cabrera, A. F., Nora, A., and Castaneda, M. B. "The Role of Finances in the Persistence Process: A Structural Model." *Research in Higher Education*, 33(5), 1993a, 571–593.

Cabrera, A. F., Nora, A., and Castaneda, M. B. "College Persistence: The Testing of an Integrated Model." *Journal of Higher Education*, 64(2), 1993b, 123–139.

Cabrera, A. F., Nora, A., Terenzini, P. T., Pascarella, E., and Hagedorn, L. S. "Campus Racial Climate and the Adjustment of Students to College." *Journal of Higher Education*, 1999, 70(2), 134–160.

Cabrera, A. F., Stampen, J. L., and Hansen, W. L. "Exploring the Effects of Ability-To-Pay on Persistence in College." *Review of Higher Education*, 1990, 13(3), 303–336.

Feldman, K., and Newcomb, T. *The Impact of College on Students.* San Francisco: Jossey-Bass, 1969.

Fleming, J. *Blacks in College: A Comparative Study of Students' Success in Black and in White Institutions.* San Francisco: Jossey-Bass, 1984.

Hall, R. H. *Organizations: Structure and Process.* Upper Saddle River, NJ: Prentice Hall, 1992.

Hurtado, S. "The Campus Racial Climate: Contexts of Conflict." *Journal of Higher Education,* 1992, *63,* 539–569.

Hurtado, S. "The Institutional Climate for Talented Latino Students." *Research in Higher Education,* 1994, *35,* 21–41.

Hurtado, S., Carter, D. F., and Spuler, A. "Latino Student Transition to College: Assessing Difficulties and Factors in Successful College Adjustment." *Research in Higher Education,* 1996, *21*(3), 279–302.

Kuh, G. D., Pace, C. R., and Vesper, N. "The Development of Process Indicators to Estimate Student Gains Associated with Good Practices in Undergraduate Education." *Research in Higher Education,* 1997, *38*(4), 435–454.

Loo, C. M., and Rolison, G. "Alienation of Ethnic Minority Students at a Predominately White University." *Journal of Higher Education,* 1986, *57,* 58–77.

Nora, A. "Determinants of Retention Among Chicano Students: A Structural Model." *Research in Higher Education,* 1987, *26*(1), 31–59.

Nora, A., and Cabrera, A. F. "The Role of Perceptions of Prejudice and Discrimination on the Adjustment of Minority Students to College." *Journal of Higher Education,* 1996, *67,* 119–148.

Pace, C. R. *Measuring the Quality of College Student Experiences.* Los Angeles: University of California, Higher Education Research Institute, 1984.

Pascarella, E. T. "College Environmental Influences on Learning and Cognitive Development: A Critical Review and Synthesis." In J. Smart (ed.), *Higher Education: Handbook of Theory and Research.* New York: Agathon, 1985.

Pascarella, E. T., and Terenzini, P. T. *How College Affects Students.* San Francisco: Jossey-Bass, 1991.

Reason, R. D., Terenzini, P. T., and Domingo, R. J. First thing's first: Developing academic competence in the first year of college. *Research in Higher Education,* 2006, *47*(2), 149–175.

Reynolds, A. L. "Working with Children and Adolescents in the Schools: Multicultural Counseling Implications." In R. H. Sheets and E. R. Hollins (eds.), *Racial and Ethnic Identity in School Practices: Aspects of Human Development.* Mahwah, NJ: Lawrence Erlbaum Associates, 1999.

Smedley, B. D., Myers, H. F., and Harrell, S. P. "Minority-Status Stresses and the College Adjustment of Ethnic Minority Freshmen." *Journal of Higher Education,* 1993, *64,* 434–452.

Spady, W. G. "Dropouts from Higher Education: An Interdisciplinary Review and Synthesis." *Interchange,* 1970, *1*(1), 64–85.

Spady, W. G. "Dropouts from Higher Education: Toward an Empirical Model." *Interchange,* 1971, *2*(3), 38–62.

St. John, E. P. "Workable Models for Institutional Research on the Impact of Student Financial Aid." *Journal of Student Financial Aid,* 1992, *22*(3), 13–26.

Stark, J., Shaw, K. and Lowther, M. (eds.). *Student Goals for College and Courses: A Missing Link in Assessing and Improving Academic Achievement.* ASHE-ERIC Higher Education Report Series, volume 18, no. 6. San Francisco: Jossey-Bass, 1989.

Strauss, L. C., and Volkwein, J. F. "Comparing Student Performance and Growth in Two-Year and Four-Year Institutions." *Research in Higher Education,* April 2002, *43,* 133–161.

Terenzini, P. T., Pascarella, E. T., and Lorang, W. "An Assessment of the Academic and Social Influences on Freshman Year Educational Outcomes." *Review of Higher Education,* 1982, *5,* 86–110.

Terenzini, P. T., and Reason, R. D. "Parsing the first year of college: A Conceptual framework for studying college impacts." Paper presented at the meeting of the Association for the Study of Higher Education, Philadelphia, PA, 2005.

NEW DIRECTIONS FOR INSTITUTIONAL RESEARCH • DOI: 10.1002/ir

Terenzini, P. T., Springer, L., Pascarella, E. T., and Nora, A. "Influences Affecting the Development of Students' Critical Thinking Skills." *Research in Higher Education*, 1995, *36*, 23–39.

Terenzini, P., Theophilides, C., and Lorang, W. "Influences on Students' Perceptions of Their Academic Skill Development During College." *Journal of Higher Education*, 1984a, *55*, 621–636.

Terenzini, P., Theophilides, C., and Lorang, W. "Influences on Students' Perception of Their Personal Development During the First Three Years of College." *Research in Higher Education*, 1984b, *21*, 178–194.

Terenzini, P., and Wright, T. "Influences on Students' Academic Growth During Four Years of College." *Research in Higher Education*, 1987a, *26*, 161–179.

Terenzini, P., and Wright, T. "Students' Personal Growth During the First Two Years of College." *Review of Higher Education*, 1987b, *10*, 259–271.

Tinto, V. *Leaving College: Rethinking the Causes and Cures of Student Attrition*. Chicago: University of Chicago Press, 1987.

Tinto, V. *Leaving College: Rethinking the Causes and Cures of Student Attrition*. (2nd ed.). Chicago: University of Chicago Press, 1993.

Toutkoushian, R. K., and Smart, J. C. "Do Institutional Characteristics Affect Student Gains from College?" *Review of Higher Education*, 2001, *25*(1), 39–61.

Upcraft, M. L., and Schuh, J. H. *Assessment in Student Affairs: A Guide for Practitioners*. San Francisco: Jossey-Bass, 1996.

Volkwein, J. F. "Improved Measures of Academic and Social Integration and Their Association with Measures of Student Growth." Paper presented at Annual Meeting of the Association for the Study of Higher Education, Boston, 1991.

Volkwein, J. F. *Albany Outcomes Model*. Albany: Office of Institutional Research, State University of New York at Albany, 1992.

Volkwein, J. F. "The Four Faces of Institutional Research." In J. F. Volkwein (ed.), *What Is Institutional Research All About: A Critical and Comprehensive Assessment of the Profession*. New Directions for Institutional Research, no. 104. San Francisco: Jossey-Bass, 1999.

Volkwein, J. F. "Using and Enhancing Existing Data to Respond to Campus Challenges." In F. K. Stage and K. Manning (eds.), *Research in the College Context: Approaches and Methods*. New York: Brunner-Routledge, 2003.

Volkwein, J. F., and Lorang, W. L. "Characteristics of Extenders: Full-time Students Who Take Light Credit Loads and Graduate in More than Four Years." *Research in Higher Education*, February 1996, *37*, 43–68.

Volkwein, J. F., King, M. C., and Terenzini, P. T. "Student Faculty Relationships and Intellectual Growth Among Transfer Students." *Journal of Higher Education*, 1986, *57*, 413–430.

Volkwein, J. F., Szelest, B., Cabrera, A., and Napierski-Prancl, M. "Factors Associated with Student Loan Default Among Different Racial and Ethnic Groups." *Journal of Higher Education*, March/April 1998, *69*, 206–237.

Volkwein, J. F., and Szelest, B. "Individual and Campus Characteristics Associated with Student Loan Default." *Research in Higher Education*, Feb. 1995, *36*, 41–72.

Volkwein, J. F., Valle, S., Blose, G., and Zhou, Y. "A Multi-Campus Study of Academic Performance and Cognitive Growth Among Native Freshman, Two-Year Transfers, and Four-Year Transfers." Paper presented at the meeting of the Association for Institutional Research Forum, Cincinnati, 2000.

Voorhees, R. A. "Student Learning and Cognitive Development in the Community College." In J. C. Smart (ed.), *Higher Education Handbook of Theory and Research* (Vol. 12). New York: Agathon Press, 1997.

Weidman, J. "Undergraduate Socialization: A Conceptual Approach." In J. Smart (ed.), *Higher Education: Handbook of Theory and Research* (Vol. 5). New York: Agathon Press, 1989.

Recommended Reading

Astin, A. "The Methodology of Research on College Impact (I) & (II)." *Sociology of Education*, 1970, *43*, 223–254, 437–450.

Astin, A. *Four Critical Years*. San Francisco: Jossey-Bass, 1977.

Burke, J. C., and Serban, A. M. (eds.). *Performance Funding for Public Higher Education: Fad or Trend?* New Directions for Institutional Research, no. 97. San Francisco: Jossey-Bass, 1998.

Cabrera, A. F., and La Nasa, S. M. "Three Critical Tasks America's Disadvantaged Face on Their Path to College." In A. F. Cabrera and S. M. La Nasa (eds.), *Understanding the College Choice of Disadvantaged Students*. New Directions for Institutional Research, no. 107. San Francisco: Jossey-Bass, 2000.

Ewell, P. T. "Identifying Indicators of Curricular Quality." In J. G. Gaff, J. L. Ratcliff, and Associates (eds.), *Handbook of the Undergraduate Curriculum: A Comprehensive Guide to Purposes, Structures, Practices, and Change*. San Francisco: Jossey-Bass, 1996.

Ewell, P. T. "National Trends in Assessing Student Learning." *Journal of Engineering Education*, 1998, *87*(2), 107–103.

Franklin, M. "The Effects of Differential College Environments on Academic Learning and Student Perceptions of Cognitive Development." *Research in Higher Education*, 1995, *36*(2), 127–154.

Metzner, B. S., and Bean, J. P. "The Estimation of a Conceptual Model of Nontraditional Undergraduate Student Attrition." *Research in Higher Education*, 1987, *27*(1), 15–38.

Middle States Commission on Higher Education. *Characteristics of Excellence in Higher Education: Eligibility Requirements and Standards for Accreditation*. (12th ed). Philadelphia: Author, 2006.

Murguia, E., Padilla, R. V., and Pavel, M. "Ethnicity and the Concept of Social Integration in Tinto's Model of Institutional Departure." *Journal of College Student Development*, 1991, *32*(5), 433–454.

Nora, A. "Campus-Based Programs as Determinants of Retention Among Hispanic College Students." *Journal of Higher Education*, 1990, *61*(3), 312–331.

Pascarella, E. T., Duby, P., and Iverson, B. "A Test and a Reconceptualization of a Theoretical Model of College Withdrawal in a Commuter Institution Setting." *Sociology of Education*, 1983, *56*, 88–100.

Pascarella, E. T., and Terenzini, P. T. "Predicting Freshman Year Persistence and Voluntary Dropout Decisions from a Theoretical Model." *Journal of Higher Education*, 1980, *51*(1), 60–75.

Pascarella, E. T., and Terenzini, P. T. "Predicting Voluntary Freshman Year Persistence/Withdrawal Behavior in a Residential University: A Path Analytic Validation of Tinto's Model." *Journal of Educational Psychology*, 1983, *75*(2), 215–226.

Peterson, M. W., and Augustine, C. H. "Organizational Practices Enhancing the Influence of Student Assessment Information in Academic Decisions." *Research in Higher Education*, 2000, *41*(1), 21–52

Porter, S. R., and Umbach, P. D. "Analyzing Faculty Workload Data Using Multilevel Modeling." *Research in Higher Education*, 2001, *42*(2), 171–197.

Ratcliff, J. L., Lubinescu, E., and Gaffney, M. (eds.) *How Accreditation Influences Assessment*. New Directions in Higher Education, no. 113. San Francisco: Jossey-Bass, 2001.

Stampen, J. O., and Cabrera, A. F. "Exploring the Effects of Student Aid on Attrition." *Journal of Financial Aid*, 1986, *16*(2), 28–39.

Terenzini, P., Pascarella, E., Theophilides, C., and Lorang, W. "A Replication of a Path Analytic Validation of Tinto's Theory of College Student Attrition." *Review of Higher Education*, 1985, *8*, 319–340.

Terenzini, P. T., and Pascarella, E. T. "Student/Faculty Relationships and Freshman Year Educational Outcomes: A Further Investigation. *Journal of College Student Personnel*, 1980, *21*, 521–528.

Terenzini, P. T., Springer, L., Yaeger, P., Pascarella, E. T., and Nora, A. "First Generation College Students: Characteristics, Experiences, and Cognitive Development." *Research in Higher Education*, 1996, 37, 1–22.

Tinto, V. "Stages of Student Departure: Reflections on the Longitudinal Characteristics of Student Leaving." *Journal of Higher Education*, 1988, 59(4), 438–455.

VanGennep, A. *The Rites of Passage* (Trans. M. Vizedon and G. Caffee). Chicago: University of Chicago Press, 1960.

Volkwein, J. F. "Assessing Institutional Effectiveness and Connecting the Pieces of a Fragmented University." In J. Burke (ed.), *Fixing the Fragmented University*. San Francisco: Jossey-Bass/Anker, 2007.

Volkwein, J. F., and Carbone, D. A. "The Impact of Departmental Research and Teaching Climates on Undergraduate Growth and Satisfaction." *Journal of Higher Education*, 1994, 65(2), 147–167.

Volkwein, J. F., Szelest, B., and Lizotte, A. "The Relationship of Campus Crime to Campus and Student Characteristics." *Research in Higher Education*, Dec. 1995, 36, 647–670.

J. FREDERICKS VOLKWEIN is emeritus professor of higher education at The Pennsylvania State University and a former director of the Center for the Study of Higher Education.

NEW DIRECTIONS FOR INSTITUTIONAL RESEARCH • DOI: 10.1002/ir

5

This chapter identifies key elements of basic skills assessment, including the advantages and disadvantages of different assessment instruments.

Basic Skills Assessment

Alexander C. Yin, J. Fredericks Volkwein

After surveying 1,827 students in their final year at eighty randomly selected two-year and four-year public and private institutions, American Institutes for Research (2006) reported that approximately 30 percent of students in two-year institutions and nearly 20 percent of students in four-year institutions have only basic quantitative literacy—the ability to compare unit prices and calculate the restaurant bill total. In 2003, the National Assessment of Adult Literacy found 14 percent and 3 percent of college graduates were, respectively, at the basic and below-basic literacy level (Kutner, Greenberg, and Baer, 2005). Basic level is the ability to read and understand short, commonplace prose texts, and below basic is the ability to locate easily identifiable information. Obviously college administrators should be worried about admitting and graduating students with only basic and below-basic skills. Basic skills assessment ensures that students both enter and graduate with skills to succeed in the world beyond the campus.

This chapter examines basic skills assessment by understanding the foundations and purposes of it, the process involved with it, and the various instruments associated with it.

What Are Basic Skills, and Why Assess Them?

There are two main purposes for basic skills assessment in higher education:

- Ensuring minimal proficiency and readiness for college-level work, especially in English literacy and numerical reasoning

New Directions for Institutional Research, Assessment Supplement 2009, Spring 2010 © Wiley Periodicals, Inc.
Published online in Wiley InterScience (www.interscience.wiley.com) • DOI: 10.1002/ir.331

- Placing students in appropriate ability levels in courses like math, music, and languages

Proficiency assessment includes English grammar and vocabulary, reading comprehension, sentence construction, written expression, and mathematics. Mathematics is usually assessed on three levels: arithmetic, elementary algebra, and college-level mathematics. Testing student understanding of grammar and sentence meaning gauges the student's proficiency level in English. Evaluating a student's writing skills can include an essay test graded on focus and clarity of the main idea, development and elaboration of the idea with supporting details, organization, sentence structure, and mechanical conventions.

Basic skills assessment provides faculty, institutional researchers, and administrators with a baseline measurement to gauge a student's progress and gains in higher education. If students have deficiencies in basic skills on entry, the institution can build these skills to ensure students have developed the necessary aptitudes to succeed in higher education and life. It is necessary, therefore, that exit proficiencies for developmental courses have an established congruence with the entrance criteria for beginning credit classes. Some of the essential motivation and uses of solid basic skills assessment include:

- Meaningful indicators of students' performance in both developmental classes and subsequent classes in the credit curriculum
- Assurances that students receiving interventions such as remedial courses perform well in subsequent college- or advanced-level course work
- Views of student satisfaction and other factors influencing student motivation and development
- Ongoing feedback for the improvement of teaching as well as student learning
- Progress relative to exit proficiencies where achievement certifies the readiness of students for college work

Basic skills assessment also gauges a student's strengths and weaknesses. Placing a student in a class he or she is not prepared for is a prescription for failure. Students placed in classes that they are overly prepared for become bored, may develop poor studying habits (they may start skipping class or sleep in class), or become a distraction to other students. In both cases, the institution and the student incur unnecessary costs.

Considerations in Developing Assessment for Basic Skills

As with all other assessment, institutional researchers and administrators need to ensure that the institution's goals and mission statement align with the basic skills assessment outcomes. Thus, tackling questions like, "Who is your university catering to?" and "Will the institution deny admission to students who do not meet the minimal basic skills level or will you provide remedial classes?" are important first steps in developing a basic skills assessment plan.

Other considerations in basic skills assessment include what tests to administer. For example, should the institution develop an instrument or use a commercially available one? (See Chapter Six, Appendix B, for the pros and cons of standardized and local instruments drawn from Ory [1991] and Volkwein [2009].) Some institutions consider student scores on the ACT or the SAT reasoning test as adequate indicators of student basic skills. Thus, if ACT is part of the application process, it may not be necessary to administer another test to measure basic skills. Standardized tests are not the only forms of assessing basic skills; life experience, work experiences, and high school grades should also be considered.

Basic Skills Assessment Tests

The remainder of this chapter describes the most commonly used commercial tests for basic skills. The section begins with a description of the most commonly used standardized tests for college admissions and placement decisions. It then provides a summary of the advantages and disadvantages of each of the other assessment instruments commonly used to assess student basic skills on campuses.

College Entrance Exams: SAT-I, SAT-II, ACT, and TOEFL

- SAT-I: http://www.collegeboard.com/student/testing/sat/about/SATI.html
- SAT-II: http://www.collegeboard.com/student/testing/sat/about/SATII.html
- ACT: http://www.act.org/aap/
- TOEFL: http://www.ets.org/portal/site/ets/menuitem.435c0b5cc7bd0ae
  7015d9510c3921509/?vgnextoid=69c0197a484f4010VgnVCM10000022f
  95190RCRD

The Scholastic Assessment Test (SAT) and American College Test (ACT) are the two most popular college entrance exams used in the college admissions process. These tests offer an assessment of a student's abilities to do well in college. They largely measure a student's abilities in math, reading, and writing. In addition, both ACT and SAT-II offer tests in science and other subjects.

The SAT. For much of its history, the SAT has been a multiple-choice test of more than three hours that measures student verbal and quantitative skills. The current SAT-I measures skills in math, critical reading, and writing. The math test is broken up into three sections for a total of seventy minutes of assessing basic algebra, geometry, and probability skills. The critical reading section is a total of seventy minutes as well. Also divided into three parts, it assesses reading comprehension based on paragraphs provided in the test. The writing section contains two parts, for a total of sixty minutes. One part is a multiple-choice exam that focuses on grammar use and word choice. The second part is an essay exam that measures a student's ability to write coherently and support an argued position. Unlike the ACT, the SAT-I does not have a science section. However, the SAT-II tests provide assessments in subject areas such as science, social studies, and foreign languages.

The SAT-II tests were created to complement the SAT and assess students in a variety of specific college-level subjects. These one-hour multiple-choice tests fall under five general areas: English (including literature), history and social studies (including U.S. and world history), math (including math 1 and math 2), science (including biology, chemistry, and physics), and languages (including Chinese, French, German, Spanish, modern Hebrew, Italian, Latin, Japanese, and Korean). Many universities require students to submit SAT-II scores depending on the major they seek. For example, students interested in math, science, or engineering are often required to take both a science subject test and the math 2 test, which assesses a student's abilities in calculus. The individual sections of the SAT-I test and the SAT-II subject tests are graded on an 800-point scale. Scores are scaled based on the national average so that the mean is close to 500. The SAT-I scales have been recentered only on a couple of occasions over the years.

The ACT. The ACT program was founded in 1959 to offer an alternative to the SAT, which at the time was the only national college entrance testing program in the United States. Moreover, for the fifty years prior to 1990, the SAT purported to measure student aptitude, whereas the ACT proposed to measure student preparation or knowledge.

Developed in Iowa City, Iowa, the ACT tests were primarily used by western and midwestern institutions until the last couple of decades, when many universities throughout the nation began accepting either SAT or ACT scores.

The ACT assesses four specific areas: English, math, reading, and science. The four tests are in multiple-choice formats and timed per section. The English test has seventy-five questions to be answered within forty-five minutes. The test measures writing and rhetorical skills. The math test has sixty questions to be answered within sixty minutes and assesses math skills up to grade level 12. The reading test has forty questions and a time limit of thirty-five minutes. It measures basic reading comprehension. Finally, the science test has forty questions to be answered in thirty-five minutes. It assesses analytical and problem-solving skills as applied to the natural sciences. Students also have an option to take the ACT writing test; it has only one question that is answered in essay format with a thirty-minute limit. This test grades college-level composition skills. Each section of the ACT test is scored out of thirty-six points. Generally students who receive a score of 28 or higher are within the top 10 percent of all students who take the test.

NEW DIRECTIONS FOR INSTITUTIONAL RESEARCH • DOI: 10.1002/ir

Evaluating the SAT and ACT. A strength of both the SAT and ACT tests is that they create standard quantitative ways of measuring student preparation that are likely to be more objective than letters from teachers and school guidance counselors, and perhaps a better indicator even than grades, which may be inflated. By assessing specific skills and areas of knowledge, universities attempt to determine in the application process the likelihood that students they admit will succeed in college.

The SAT and ACT tests have long been criticized for being skewed against minority students. However, most studies suggest that curricular rigor, family income, and family encouragement are more important than race in explaining student performance (Adelman, 1989, 1999, 2004; Cabera and La Nasa, 2000; Thomas, 2004).

The TOEFL. The Test of English as a Foreign Language (TOEFL) measures the ability of nonnative speakers of English to use and understand English as it is spoken, written, and heard in college and university settings. The test is offered in three formats: Internet based, computer based, and paper based. The Internet-based test assesses student ability in speaking, listening, reading, and writing. The computer-based TOEFL measures English language proficiency in listening, structure, reading, and writing. The paper-based test measures students' ability in listening, comprehension, structure and written expression, and reading comprehension.

Credit by Exams: AP and CLEP

- AP: http://www.ets.org/portal/site/ets/menuitem.c988ba0e5dd572bada20 bc47c3921509/?vgnextoid=1b0daf5e44df4010VgnVCM10000022f95190R CRD&vgnextchannel=ba6de3b5f64f4010VgnVCM10000022f95190RCRD
- CLEP: http://www.collegeboard.com/student/testing/clep/exams.html

For college-bound high school students, taking advanced college-level courses has become a dominant feature of the high school curriculum. Although there are multiple ways to transfer these college-level courses to credits at the university a student attends, the most popular is through the Advanced Placement (AP) and College Level Examination Program (CLEP) offered by the College Board. By taking tests in specific subject areas and performing well, students can receive university credit.

AP. In 1951, a group of high school and university administrators formed a committee to publish a report known as the *General Education in School and College.* In the report, the committee (including administrators from Princeton, Yale, and Harvard) called for advanced high school course work to be available to students in their last two years of high school. These courses would not only offer a chance for high school students to explore various college-level subject areas but also allow students to experience college-level classes that could count for university credit.

In 1955, the College Board began running the program, and since then, tests have expanded to thirty-five exams in twenty subject areas, including calculus, computer science, economics, English, government (comparative, U.S.), history (art, European, U.S., World), language (French, German, Italian, Latin, Spanish), human geography, music theory, psychology, science (biology, chemistry, environmental, physics), statistics, and studio art. Each test, generally multiple choice (English is essay based), is graded on a five-point scale, with 5 considered the highest. Students who score at least a 3 are considered to have the ability to pass the equivalent college course. However, most universities will accept only a 4 or 5 for credit.

The original focus of the AP and CLEP exams was to offer students early preparation for college. AP courses supposedly offer college rigor, such as a more challenging curriculum, more study hours, and harder exams. In addition, they give high schools the opportunity to offer students courses beyond those traditional for secondary education. Students can explore areas such as accounting, economics, or environmental science to determine early on whether they are interested in the discipline. Students using the AP and CLEP tests wisely can start college with a better understanding of the subjects they are and are not interested in.

Students who take an AP course do not necessarily exercise their option to take the AP test. Multiple factors have produced dramatic increases in the number of students enrolling in AP courses. In the past decade, students taking and passing AP courses have tripled in some states and increased sixfold in others. Studies have shown a positive correlation between taking AP courses and college graduation rates. Moreover, students and their families are competing for admission to the top colleges and responding to the need to look better in the college admissions process, as well as to shorten the number of years of tuition payment. AP courses increase the perceived strength of a student's high school course load, which can help in the admissions process (Marklein, 2006). Thus, secondary schools face pressure to offer courses in a variety of AP subjects.

College faculty and administrators are reconsidering their AP standards and whether students passing the tests are as prepared as they should be. Many believe that high school AP courses may focus on helping students pass the exam rather than focusing on learning the subject material. Educators also worry about the disadvantage some students have based on the high school they attend. Schools in lower-income areas are less likely to offer a wide variety of AP courses. In addition, students who do take the AP course may not be able to afford the test, let alone multiple tests. While some students find themselves unable to take AP courses, other students find themselves taking as many as possible. Within the past decade, the number of students taking nine or more AP exams has increased more than sixfold. Although the number of racial and ethnic minority students taking AP tests is increasing, they still lag behind their white counterparts (Dixon, 2006; Mathews, 2006).

NEW DIRECTIONS FOR INSTITUTIONAL RESEARCH • DOI: 10.1002/ir

CLEP. CLEP exams are similar to AP tests in that universities use scores on CLEP to determine if a student should receive credit for a college-level course. Unlike the AP, CLEP does not offer an equivalent course for students to take. Whereas the AP program offers both courses and tests that help students understand the rigors of college learning, CLEP is simply a test offered to students. To prepare, students have the option of studying on their own or taking courses through adult learner programs, community colleges, or the armed services. CLEP is popular among military personnel, in part because the Defense Activity for Non-Traditional Education Support funds CLEP exams for military personnel who wish to take them.

CLEP exam subjects are wide ranging, similar to the APs, and include composition and literature (American literature, analyzing and interpreting literature, English composition, English literature, freshman college composition, humanities), foreign languages (French, German, Spanish), history and social sciences (American government, human growth and development, educational psychology, psychology, sociology, economics, U.S. history, Western civilization), science and math (biology, calculus, chemistry, college algebra, natural science, precalculus, college math), and business (accounting, business law, information systems and computer applications, management, marketing).

CLEP exams are ninety minutes in length, primarily comprising multiple-choice questions and some fill-in-the-blank. The English composition exam does have a written essay portion. CLEP test scores range up to 80 points, and for most subjects, a score of 50 is equivalent to passing the equivalent college-level course; however, universities may increase or decrease the required score for granting credit.

Commonly Used Instruments for Assessing Basic Skills: ACCU-PLACER, ASSET, COMPASS/ESL, and Nelson-Denny

- ACCUPLACER: http://professionals.collegeboard.com/higher-ed/placement/accuplacer
- ASSET: http://www.act.org/asset/tests/index.html
- COMPASS/ESL: http://www.act.org/compass/index.html
- Nelson-Denny: http://www.riverpub.com/products/ndrt/index.html

ACCUPLACER. ACCUPLACER is a suite of computer-adaptive tests in reading comprehension, sentence skills, arithmetic, elementary algebra, and college-level mathematics, including English as a Second Language (ESL) assessment. The writing assessment test, WritePlacer, electronically scores writing samples using artificial intelligence. These nationally normed tests for incoming college students provide a quick and accurate determination of whether a student has the skills to take a freshman course or would benefit from developmental work.

ACCUPLACER Online claims to be the first computer-adaptive placement testing program delivered over the Internet. As summarized in the Appendix at the end of this chapter, computer-adaptive tests adjust to the level of each student being tested by delivering subsequent questions based on the difficulty level of the questions the student answers. ACCUPLACER allows large numbers of students to be assessed simultaneously at relatively low cost because there is no need to deal with network installations, upgrades, and maintenance. Scoring is immediate, with individual student reports that contain course placement information. Any site with Internet access and a proctor can function as a test center, including libraries, local high schools, the campus placement center, and satellite campuses. ACCUPLACER can be used to conduct off-site orientation programs for new students in several locations and allows colleges to work with feeder high schools to assess the academic readiness of student applicants.

ACCUPLACER Pros
- ACCUPLACER is a useful tool for placing students in the correct courses for their skill level in reading, writing, math, and ESL.
- ACCUPLACER shares the advantages of nationally designed standardized tests, yet fewer of the disadvantages because it is available online at lower cost, with the results and scores immediately available.
- Writing samples are scored electronically, eliminating the need to read and grade hundreds of essays by hand.
- The tests can be taken at remote locations with a proctor.
- If the tests are taken remotely prior to orientation, placement test results are available when the students arrive on campus and meet with their advisors at orientation.
- Scores can be exported into campus information systems.

ACCUPLACER Cons
- Although computer adaptive testing is convenient and allows the test to be shorter, it is not possible to use the scores in a statistical analysis because the test takers do not answer the same questions or take tests that are the same difficulty level. It is true that the difficulty of the items answered is built into the scoring; nevertheless, using all of the students' scores in a regression analysis may not be appropriate because the students' tests are not the same.
- Thus, comparing the outcomes of students with their scores is not appropriate, because they may have gotten different types of questions wrong.
- Having the exams proctored at sites such as high schools may be convenient; however, some test sites may be more honestly proctored than others. In situations where the school will look bad if many of their students perform poorly, some coaching could be occurring during the exam.
- A locally developed test may better represent exactly what the faculty at a particular institution need to know for proper student placement in courses.

NEW DIRECTIONS FOR INSTITUTIONAL RESEARCH • DOI: 10.1002/ir

ASSET. ASSET is a series of three placement tests, using a multiple-choice format, of basic skills in writing, reading, and numerical reasoning. More advanced tests in algebra and geometry are also available. Test scores indicate students' strengths and weaknesses within the subject—information that helps institutions to guide students toward classes that will strengthen and build logically on their current knowledge and skills.

The ASSET Writing Skills Test measures a student's understanding of appropriate use in grammar, punctuation, sentence structure, writing strategy, and writing style. It does not, however, test spelling, vocabulary, or recall of more basic memorized grammar rules. Three types of prose passages are given, each accompanied by twelve multiple-choice questions.

The reading skills test consists of three passages in different fields written at the college freshman level. Each passage has eight questions: four pertaining to reading comprehension and four that require the student to make logical inferences that extend beyond text information.

The numerical skills test consists of thirty-two questions to be answered without a calculator and assesses knowledge and skills in the performance of basic math operations using whole numbers, decimals, and fractions. This test also measures prealgebra knowledge and skills such as the understanding of prime numbers, absolute values, scientific notation, and square roots. The elementary algebra test measures skills often taught in a first-year high school algebra class, including evaluating and simpli-fying algebraic expressions, solving linear and quadratic equations, and performing operations with polynomials. The intermediate algebra test measures topics often taught in a second year high school algebra class, including factoring, graphing, solving linear inequalities, and calculating slope distance. The college algebra test measures skills often taught in a first-year college algebra course, including performing operations with complex numbers, exponential functions, factorials, and graphs of polynomials. The geometry test measures skills often taught in a high school geometry class, including understanding formulas and principles related to squares, triangles, circles, and other geometrical figures.

The three scoring options are self-scoring, machine scoring using a stand-alone scanner, and computer scoring. All three offer an immediate printout of the customized ASSET Student Advising Report containing course placement information.

ASSET Pros

- The math exam extends through college-level algebra.
- The test is not computer adaptive; every student takes the same exam.
- Score cut-offs for course placement can be adjusted.
- The Entering Students Descriptive Report provides useful information about the needs of newly enrolling students and compares them to students across the country who have completed ASSET testing.
- The Returning Students Retention Report provides course completion and reenrollment information for tested students.

- An extra feature, the Course Placement Service, provides analyses that can be used to evaluate whether students are being placed in the correct courses and whether the score cut-offs are appropriate.
- The Student Advising Report is ready immediately.
- ASSET data can be uploaded to the campus system, so it can be used for analytical purposes.
- ASSET has query capabilities for generating lists, mailing labels, and letters.

ASSET Cons

- Tests must be taken on-site, so there is no opportunity to have students tested prior to their arrival on campus.
- There is no ESL component.
- Because the exams are not computer adaptive, fewer questions are targeted to a particular student's level. For example, students at the lowest level may not be able to complete large sections of the test and have only a few questions pertaining to information they know.
- There is no written essay exam.

COMPASS/ESL. The Computerized Adaptive Placement Assessment and Support System (COMPASS)/ESL provides measures of key skills useful for placing students in writing, reading, and mathematics or into ESL courses.

The COMPASS mathematics test is a multiple-choice test that assesses students in basic skills (performing a sequence of basic operations), application (applying sequences of basic operations to novel settings or in complex ways), and analysis (demonstrating conceptual understanding of principles and relationships in mathematical operations). The five mathematics placement tests are in numerical skills/prealgebra, algebra, college algebra, geometry, and trigonometry.

The writing skills placement test helps institutions determine a student's ability to find and correct errors in essays, including punctuation, basic grammar and use, sentence structure, and rhetorical skills, which include strategy, organization, and style.

The ESL component has three tests: grammar/usage, reading, and listening. The grammar/usage test assesses the ability to recognize and manipulate standard American English in two main areas: sentence elements and sentence structure and syntax. The reading test assesses the ability to recognize and manipulate standard American English in two categories: referring (reading explicitly stated material) and reasoning (inferential reading). The listening test assesses the ability to understand standard American English.

COMPASS/ESL Pros

- The COMPASS/ESL Internet Version reaches both locally and geographically dispersed students.
- COMPSS/ESL is untimed, eliminating time pressures and reducing student anxiety. This is particularly important for ESL students.

New Directions for Institutional Research • DOI: 10.1002/ir

- Schools using COMPASS can incorporate the student profile question-naire into their data collection processes.
- The ESL tests in the COMPASS system have been approved by the U.S. Department of Education for use in determining student eligibility for Title IV financial aid funding through the ability-to-benefit requirements and procedures that went into effect on May 19, 2006. (See http://www .act.org/compass/advant/atb.html.)
- COMPASS/ESL can reach foreign and disabled students.
- COMPASS/ESL can be used when nonnative speakers score below a given range on the TOEFL, to assess for placement in ESL classes.

COMPASS/ESL Cons
- It has disadvantages inherent in computer testing (see the Appendix).
- The test is appropriate for reading, writing, and math skills but not for critical thinking or problem solving.

Nelson-Denny Reading Test. Riverside Publishing's Nelson-Denny Reading Test, Forms G and H, is a reading test for high school and college students and adults. The Nelson-Denny measures vocabulary development, comprehension, and reading rate. The thirty-five-minute test is broken into two parts. Part I (Vocabulary) is a fifteen-minute test; part II (Comprehension and Rate) is a twenty-minute test. The first minute of the comprehension test determines the reading rate of the tester, including the time needed to distribute materials, complete the name and information grids, and provide directions. The test may be administered in forty-five minutes or a single class period. There is also an extended version of the test that takes fifty-six minutes to administer for ESL students. The cost depends on the size of the order and whether both forms are purchased. To administer and score fifty tests (either Form G or H) costs about twelve dollars per student.

Nelson-Denny Pros
- The two equated versions of the test allow a pretest/posttest assessment methodology.
- Forms G and H have been equated (compatible/comparative) to earlier versions of the test (Forms E and F).
- The test is quick to administer.
- An extended-time test version is available for ESL students.

Nelson-Denny Cons
- Manual scoring by the institution (no external service for scoring tests).
- Limited norm-referencing capability for peer comparisons (national norms only).
- No aggregate reporting.
- Support offered only with an online form.

Appendix: Advantages and Disadvantages of Adaptive Computerized Testing

Advantages
- Provides increased assessment accuracy with fewer items and less time.
- Eliminates the need for test booklets and answer sheets.
- Test results can be available immediately to make course placement and advising decisions.
- Allows flexible walk-in testing, with individualized start and finish times.
- The tests are not timed, helping to relieve the stress and fatigue of students who are testing in a second language or are computer novices.
- The computer routes students to appropriate levels based on their test responses. Beginning students are not required to sit through questions for which they have no background, and advanced students are not forced to answer many items that are too easy.
- Valuable student demographic data can be gathered during the testing process.
- A best practice provides feedback during the test (NPEC Sourcebook on Assessment, Volume 2, http://nces.ed.gov/pubsearch/pubsinfo.asp?pubid= 2000196).

Disadvantages
- Difficult to create notes and scribble explanations on the test.
- When screens show only one question at a time, test takers cannot skip ahead and move on past difficult questions or use the test-taking technique of skipping questions and then coming back to them.
- When students cannot change or review previously answered questions, careless errors cannot be corrected, leading to lower scores.
- Students who are more comfortable with computers have an advantage over those who have not had much experience using computers.
- Computer hardware and software is expensive. Some schools have hardware limitations regarding the number of computers that are available, and items that may use graphs or detailed artwork are hard to present using older computers.
- Computer technology staff are needed to build and maintain the computer systems and software at testing sites. The cost of technology is especially problematic for colleges and universities in second and third world countries.
- Access by the physically impaired may be a problem.

References

Adelman, C. *Signs and Traces*. Washington, DC: U.S. Department of Education, 1989.

Adelman, C. *Answers in the Tool Box: Academic Intensity, Attendance Patterns, and Bachelor's Degree Attainment*. Washington, DC: U.S. Department of Education, 1999.

Adelman, C. *The Empirical Curriculum*. Washington, DC: U.S. Department of Education, 2004.

American Institutes for Research. "Fact Sheet: The National Survey of America's College Students." 2006. Retrieved May 23, 2008, from http://www.air.org/news/documents/collegeliteracyfactsheet.htm.

Cabrera, A. F., and La Nasa, S. M. (eds.). *Understanding the College Choice of Disadvantaged Students*. New Directions in Institutional Research, no. 107. San Francisco: Jossey-Bass, 2000.

Dixon, F. "Differentiating Instruction in AP: An Important Question? Or, out of the Question?" *Gifted Child Today*, 2006, *29*(2), 50–54.

Kutner, M., Greenberg, E., and Baer, J. *A First Look at the Literacy of America's Adults in the 21st Century*. Jessup, MD: U.S. Department of Education, 2005.

Marklein, M. B. "Amassing Advanced Coursework: An 'Arms Race' Among Students." *USA Today*, Mar. 21, 2006, p. D2.

Mathews, J. "Why AP Matters, Test Wars." *Newsweek*, May 8, 2006, p. 63.

Ory, J. C. "Suggestions for Deciding Between Commercially Available and Locally Developed Assessment Instruments." *NCA Quarterly*, 1991, *66*(2), 451–457.

Thomas, K. M. "The SAT II: Minority/Majority Test-Score Gaps and What They Could Mean for College Admissions." *Social Science Quarterly*, 2004, *85*(5), 1318–1331.

Volkwein, J. F. "AIR Assessment Workshop." Presented at the Annual Meeting of AIR in Atlanta, May 2009.

Recommended Reading

Arenson, K. W. "Officials Say Scoring Errors for SAT Were Understated." *New York Times*, Mar. 9, 2006, p. A18.

Holsendolph, E. "New Test, Same Problems." *Black Issues in Higher Education*, June 2, 2005, pp. 26–29.

Manzo, K. K. "Most States Earn Poor Grades for World-History Standards." *Education Week*, June 14, 2006, p. 12.

Silverstein, S., and Trounson, R. "UCLA, Cal Rejections Baffle High SAT Scorers." *Los Angeles Times*, Nov. 20, 2003, p. A1.

ALEXANDER C. YIN *is a senior project associate of the Center for the Study of Higher Education at The Pennsylvania State University.*

J. FREDERICKS VOLKWEIN *is emeritus professor of higher education at The Pennsylvania State University and a former director of the Center for the Study of Higher Education.*

6

*This chapter identifies key elements of general education
assessment, including the advantages and disadvantages
of different approaches and the available instruments.*

Assessing General Education Outcomes

Alexander C. Yin, J. Fredericks Volkwein

In both purpose and practice, general education in American higher education has experienced several recurring debates and national revivals (Boyer and Levine, 1981; Lattuca and Stark, 2009). Should students have a vocational or a liberal education, specialized or broad, applied or general? Shifting attitudes toward a general or liberal education have stimulated curricular shifts. In 1967, the average proportion of general education credits needed for a baccalaureate degree was 43.1 percent (Ratcliff, Johnson, La Nasa, and Gaff, 2001). However, as education became more specialized, the general education requirement decreased. The general education requirements began to increase only within the past two decades, with organizations like the Association of American Colleges and Universities (AAC&U) calling for reforms.

With globalization and technology equalizing a country's ability to compete economically and industrially, well-rounded graduates are better prepared to succeed in Friedman's (2006) "flat world." The AAC&U (2004a) answers the question best: "In today's knowledge-based economy, a good liberal education embraces science and new technologies, hands-on research, global knowledge, teamwork, cross-cultural learning, active engagement with the world beyond the academy, and a commitment to life-long learning, as well as the acquisition of knowledge and skills" (p. 4).

In a world with constantly evolving technology, students need a strong general education to be flexible and adaptable to the changes of the world. Job loyalty is a concept of the past, reflected in how often people change not

NEW DIRECTIONS FOR INSTITUTIONAL RESEARCH, Assessment Supplement 2009, Spring 2010 © Wiley Periodicals, Inc.
Published online in Wiley InterScience (www.interscience.wiley.com) • DOI: 10.1002/ir.332

only jobs but also careers. Having a practical or specialized education may not be enough to succeed today.

Even careers once considered specialized require people to have a strong foundation in a variety of subjects. For example, automobile mechanics need to both understand the mechanics of a car and have a firm grasp on electronics as cars have become increasingly more complex with computers built into them.

Higher education institutions are now facing constant pressure for accountability on student outcomes from parents, trustees, and the government. Institutional research can play an important role in aiding higher education leaders in fulfilling the demands for student assessment and accountability. In order to accomplish these difficult feats, institutional researchers must understand both what is being taught to students and how to evaluate their newly obtained knowledge and skills. General education is an important component and requirement of a student's education; thus, institutional researchers ought to understand its dynamics.

This chapter first examines and compares the definitions of general education published by the Association of American Colleges and Universities and the six regional accrediting agencies. We then describe issues and challenges surrounding general education assessment and conclude by identifying general education assessment methods, measures, and instruments.

What Is General Education?

The AAC&U has undertaken a decade-long campaign to focus national attention on the deteriorating state of general education. By conducting studies of high school and college students, faculty, employers, civic leaders, and accrediting bodies, it has galvanized a national consensus and hopes to provoke constructive change.

Earlier in this decade, the AAC&U published *Greater Expectations: A New Vision for Learning as a Nation Goes to College* (2002) and *Taking Responsibility for the Quality of the Baccalaureate Degree* (2004a) derived from its studies and from a diverse panel of corporate, government, and education stakeholders. In these and other reports (2004b, 2005), the AAC&U has identified a set of college student outcomes that today's citizens need (see Table 6.1). Figuring prominently in this list of necessary survival skills are cross-disciplinary perspectives and intercultural knowledge, verbal and written communication skills, analytical and problem-solving skills, collaboration and teamwork, information literacy, integrative thinking, and civic responsibility.

The AAC&U list of desired outcomes in 2004 echoes those articulated earlier by Stark and Lowther in their report, "Strengthening the Ties That Bind" (1988), in which they identified the student outcomes that higher education should promote in order to integrate professional education and the liberal arts. Table 6.1 shows the parallels among these recommended lib-

Table 6.1. Higher Education and Industry Consensus on Liberal Education Outcomes

	Stark and Lowther (1988)	*AAC&U (2004)*
Knowledge of human culture and the natural world	Professional identity Aesthetic sensibility	Understanding and experience with the inquiry practices of disciplines that explore the natural, social, and cultural realms: natural sciences, social sciences, arts, and humanities
Intellectual and practical skills	Communication competence Adaptive competence Scholarly concern for improvement Critical thinking Leadership capacity	Written and verbal communication skills Quantitative and analytical skills Information literacy Teamwork and problem-solving skills Integrative thinking and the ability to transfer skills and knowledge from one setting to another
Individual and social responsibility	Contextual competence Professional ethics Motivation for continued learning	Intercultural knowledge and collaborative skills Proactive sense of responsibility for civic, individual, and social choices.

eral education outcomes according to the combined judgments of an array of national stakeholders in both 1988 and 2004.

Unfortunately the various regional accreditation bodies do not reflect this national consensus in their accreditation standards. The integrative work of the AAC&U is not particularly visible in the accreditation standards of the major accrediting bodies. Each has its own definition of general education and separate sets of expected outcomes.

The six regional accrediting agencies define general education in the following ways:

> The institution's curricula are designed so that students acquire and demonstrate college-level proficiency in general education and essential skills, including at least oral and written communication, scientific and quantitative reasoning, critical analysis and reasoning, and technological competency. [Middle States Commission on Higher Education 2006, p. 47].

> General education embodies the institution's definition of an educated person and prepares students for the world in which they will live. . . .The general education requirement in each undergraduate program ensures adequate

breadth for all degree-seeking students by showing a balanced regard for what are traditionally referred to as the arts and humanities, the sciences including mathematics, and the social sciences. General education requirements include offerings that focus on the subject matter and methodologies of these three primary domains of knowledge as well as on their relationships to one another. . . . Graduates successfully completing an undergraduate program demonstrate competence in written and oral communication in English; the ability for scientific and quantitative reasoning, for critical analysis and logical thinking; and the capability for continuing learning, including the skills of information literacy. They also demonstrate knowledge and understanding of scientific, historical, and social phenomena, and a knowledge and appreciation of the aesthetic and ethical dimensions of humankind. [New England Association of Schools and Colleges, 2005, pp. 4.15–4.18].

The general education component of the institution's degree programs is based on a rationale that is clearly articulated and is published in clear and complete terms in the catalog. It provides the criteria by which the relevance of each course to the general education component is evaluated. . . . The general education program offerings include the humanities and fine arts, the natural sciences, mathematics, and the social sciences. The program may also include courses that focus on the interrelationships between these major fields of study. [North Central Association of Colleges and Schools, 2003, p. 30].

General education introduces students to the content and methodology of the major areas of knowledge—the humanities and fine arts, the natural sciences, mathematics, and the social sciences—and helps them develop the mental skills that will make them more effective learners [Northwest Commission on Colleges and Universities, 2003, p. 36].

In each undergraduate degree program, the institution requires the successful completion of a general education component at the collegiate level that (1) is a substantial component of each undergraduate degree, (2) ensures breadth of knowledge, and (3) is based on a coherent rationale. . . . These credit hours are to be drawn from and include at least one course from each of the following areas: humanities/fine arts, social/behavioral sciences, and natural science/mathematics. [Southern Association of Colleges and Schools, 2008, p. 17].

Baccalaureate programs engage students in an integrated course of study of sufficient breadth and depth to prepare them for work, citizenship, and in fulfilling life. These programs also ensure the development of core learning abilities and competencies including but not limited to, college-level written and oral communication; college-level quantitative skills; informational literacy;

and the habit of critical analysis of data and argument. In addition, baccalaureate programs actively foster an understanding of diversity; civic responsibility; the ability to work with others; and the capability to engage in lifelong learning. Baccalaureate programs also ensure breadth for all students in the areas of cultural and aesthetic, social and political, as well as scientific and technical knowledge expected of educated persons in this society [Western Association of Schools and Colleges, 2008, p. 14].

Although none of the regional accrediting bodies has general education language that is exactly aligned with the AAC&U principles, the standards articulated by the Middle States, New England, and Western associations come close. According to their Web sites, the North Central Northwest associations make general education sound like a distribution requirement across the arts and humanities, math and sciences, and social sciences. The Southern Association requires only that general education be a substantial, broad, and coherent component of each student's undergraduate program. Thus, the regional accrediting bodies are not completely in sync with the work of the AAC&U. Inconsistent language can only impede general education assessment efforts. Bringing more consistent language to the general education discourse offers at least a partial contribution to fixing the fragmented university at the undergraduate level (Volkwein, 2007).

Since we appear to have a national consensus among business, government, and accreditation leaders about the liberal education outcomes that all undergraduates should possess, perhaps institutional researchers should work with faculty to encourage the development of these key educational outcomes as explicit institutional and curricular objectives. Why should not all faculty members engaged in undergraduate instruction build these outcomes into each appropriate course?

The AAC&U consensus outcomes suggest that faculty members ought to grade students on what they actually know rather than other factors, like improvement, effort, or comparison. In the meantime, however, enhanced general education assessment within each course provides students with better information and makes them more introspective about their own learning, and it can encourage faculty to be more thoughtful and precise about their feedback to students, which is, after all, a component of student learning. Moreover, enhanced grading within each course should be combined with greater clarity up front as well. Faculty not only need to define those whom the course is intended to serve, but also to describe what is to be learned and whether it is intended to contribute to the student's specialized or general knowledge. Course-level assessment of liberal education outcomes places the ownership of student learning assessment back in the hands of faculty, where it belongs. Such an assessment system may be much more cost-effective than the current disjointed assessment efforts that faculty feel so far removed from.

Implementing a Program of Assessment for General Education

Several authors (Volkwein and Bauer, 2002; Bauer, 2003; Volkwein, 2009) have discussed five key steps in assessment:

1. Specify the purposes, goals, and audiences.
2. Design methods and measures.
3. Carry out the data collection and analysis.
4. Communicate the findings to the audience.
5. Obtain feedback, follow-up, redesign, and improvement.

These five steps have been incorporated into the Volkwein model for assessing institutional effectiveness described in Chapter Two. In the specific context of general education assessment, the institution and its general education committee need to define the expected general education outcomes within the context of the school's mission and appropriate accrediting agencies. Articulating clear purposes, learning goals, and assessment audiences lay good foundations for any assessment program. As discussed in Chapter Two, those conducting the assessment need to decide what question or questions are to be addressed. For example, what are the desired learning goals, and are students meeting them? How important is the measurement of improvement over time, and does the evidence suggest that student growth is occurring? How important is the assessment of individual learners versus the assessment of programs and the institution as a whole? Once institutions have defined these parameters, they need to design the appropriate methods and measures. Once the design phase is complete, they must collect data, analyze them, and communicate the findings. The feedback loop includes decisions about altering the mission statement, improving the assessment measures, clarifying institutional goals and program objectives, as well as altering programs and improving student outcomes.

Figure 6.1 integrates these five key assessment steps with the Volkwein effectiveness model discussed in Chapter Two and the discussion by Terenzini in Chapter Three.

There are two challenges most commonly encountered in general education assessment programs. The first of these has already been discussed above, namely identifying and agreeing on general education goals. As noted earlier, the AAC&U *Greater Expectations* national panel recommended the skill sets that all students need to succeed in the twenty-first century, and it did this by defining what the intentional learner should know and be able to do (see Appendix A). An assessment committee can use these descriptors in targeting desired outcomes for the general education assessment plan.

In addition, the accountability questions (see page 86) provided by the AAC&U (2004b, p. 8) may help to focus the general education assessment plan's purposes and goals.

NEW DIRECTIONS FOR INSTITUTIONAL RESEARCH • DOI: 10.1002/ir

Figure 6.1. General Education Assessment Process

Mission and Vision General Education Outcomes

1) **Specify the purposes, goals, and audience.**
2) **Design methods and measures.**

Objects of Assessment	Are we meeting our goals?	Are we improving?
Individual	College-Level Examination Program—General Defining Issues Test Watson Glaser Critical Thinking Test Locally designed tests and essays Portfolios, simulations, performances External examiners Archival records and interviews Classroom research Interviews and focus groups	All pre/posttests Classroom research Interviews and focus groups
Group	ACT Collegiate Assessment of Academic Proficiency ACT Surveys of student and alumni outcomes Collegiate Learning Assessment ETS Proficiency Profile—MAPP Classroom research Interviews and focus groups	College BASE ACT Collegiate Assessment of Academic Proficiency ETS Proficiency Profile—MAPP ACT Surveys of student and alumni outcomes Self-reported growth Classroom research Interviews and focus groups

3) **Carry out the data collection and analysis.**

4) **Communicate the findings to Stakeholders.**

5) **Obtain feedback, follow-up, redesign, and improve.**

Enhance Mission Statement	Improve Assessment Measures
Clarify Goals and Objectives	Alter Programs and Improve Student Outcomes

Are all students expected to produce advanced, culminating work?

Is this culminating work assessed for broad [general] education outcomes as well as knowledge relevant to a specific field?

Have standards been established and made public for what is expected at this advanced level in each program?

Are examples of this advanced work and the related standards regularly peer reviewed in the context of accreditation?

Have milestone assessments been established that prepared students to meet advanced standards and, where relevant, to plan for successful transfer from one institution to another?

Does the curriculum effectively prepare students to meet the standards that will be expected in milestone and culminating assessments?

General Education Assessment Methods. In the remainder of this chapter, including the appendixes, we assist the reader by addressing the second great assessment challenge, namely the selection of appropriate assessment methods and instruments.

Most campuses face a choice between two alternatives: (1) adopting a required curricular structure that ensures student attainment of the stated general education objectives or (2) collecting outcomes assessment evidence that students are achieving these things on graduation. In other words, we need either to strengthen educational requirements on the front end or to develop a system for accumulating and reflecting on outcomes evidence on the back end of the student experience.

Please note that Figure 6.1 above classifies several assessment methods and instruments on two dimensions: (1) whether they are more appropriate for assessing general education outcomes for individual students or for groups of students (such as freshmen, transfers, seniors, males, females, athletes); and (2) whether they are more appropriate for measuring goal attainment or improvement.

Tebo-Messina and Prus (1995) describe eleven methods that can be used for general education assessment: (1) commercial standardized exams, (2) locally developed exams (including essays), (3) simulation or performance appraisals, (4) written surveys and questionnaires, (5) interviews and focus groups, (6) external examiners, (7) archival records and transcript analysis, (8) portfolios, (9) behavioral observations, (10) student self-evaluations, and (11) classroom research. Appendix B describes the pros and cons of these approaches; however, a combination of methods, not just one, is usually necessary for an effective and informative assessment of general education.

You may notice in Appendix B that all of these assessment strategies except two are locally developed. The two exceptions are using external examiners and administering commercial standardized tests. Although faculty should have a strong voice in selecting external examiners and tests, faculty judgments about general education outcomes are at least partially surrendered in both cases. Institutional researchers are rarely involved in the selection of external examiners. This is most often an academic exercise carried out by deans, chairs, and program heads. The goal is to find the right balance of qualifications, familiarity, and detachment. Geographical location and cost usually figure into the decision mix.

Commercial Options for Assessing General Education. Institutional researchers frequently find that they are expected to serve as resource experts for campus assessment programs. In particular, general education committees often need advice about commercial tests that are available. We review here some of the most widely used.

ACT's Collegiate Assessment of Academic Proficiency. Institutions have the flexibility to customize their assessment needs for general education by using any combination of six test modules from the Collegiate Assessment of Academic Proficiency (CAAP; http://www.act.org/caap/index.html). The modules include multiple-choice tests for reading, writing skills, mathematics, science, and critical thinking and an essay test to evaluate writing essays. Each test is nationally standardized and lasts forty minutes. With multiple forms of each test, institutions can assess programs by using either a cross-sectional method or a longitudinal design (by readministering the CAAP or linking the results to ACT or COMPASS tests).

To allow a more finely grained analysis in assessing a program's strengths and weaknesses, CAAP provides a total score and a subscore for the Writing Skills Test (use and rhetorical skills), the Reading Test (arts/literature and social/natural sciences), and the Mathematics Test (basic and college algebra). ACT also provides institutions with the flexibility to add nine locally developed questions to any of the multiple-choice tests. It then provides the frequency distribution for each of these items. The Writing Essay Test is assessed on a scale of 1 to 6 in 0.5 increments, where responses are evaluated on student's ability to state a position and support the argument in a logical manner. The following link provides sample questions for each test: http://www.act.org/caap/sample/index.html.

ACT College Outcomes Survey. ACT's Evaluation Survey Services (ESS; http://www.act.org/ess/index.html) allows institutions to purchase the company's standardized surveys and scoring/reporting services, or alternatively, to use ACT's expertise in developing customized surveys for program evaluation. ACT has standardized surveys for two-year (www.act.org/ess/twoyear.html) and four-year colleges (www.act.org/ess/fouryear.html) that collect information on students' and alumni perceived needs, perceptions of their development, and the institution's influence on their development. Several of these ACT surveys are useful for evaluating student needs, student services, student support programs, and facilities, but are most appropriate for measuring student inputs and needs, rather than outcomes. Exceptions include the ACT College Outcomes Survey (http://www.act.org/ess/pdf/CollegeOutcomes.pdf) and the ACT Alumni Surveys which contain a mix of self-reported outcomes and evaluations of the undergraduate experience, including an array of items for assessing general education. The College Outcomes Survey in particular contains over 40 items reflecting students' personal and intellectual growth. The information collected on these surveys is self-reported, subject to the limitations described in Chapter Ten, and thus a less direct measure of general education skills than the data collected from tests such as CAAP and the others listed here.

College BASE. The Assessment Resource Center (ARC) at the University of Missouri developed the College BASE in the 1980s (http://arc.missouri.edu/index.php?p=/CB/CBN/CBoutsideMO_InstInfo.htm). Over 135 institutions have used this criterion-referenced exam to evaluate individuals for teacher education programs or to test general academic knowledge and skills. College BASE is a multiple-choice test that assesses students' English, mathematics, science, and social studies skills. Part of the assessment can include an optional essay. Institutions also have the option of customizing the test to select any combination of the four subject areas to assess or construct a short-form version of the test. One short-form design randomly assigns students to only one or two subject areas, but provides the institution with aggregate information on all four subject areas.

College Board's College-Level Examination Program. The College-Level Examination Program (CLEP; http://www.collegeboard.com/student/testing/clep/exams.html) provides exams in subject areas that students normally complete in their first two years of college. Subject areas are within composition and literature, foreign languages, history and social sciences, science and mathematics, and business. Each exam is ninety minutes, and except for the English composition test with essay, the majority of the exam items are multiple choice. Generally these tests are given to individuals seeking to demonstrate their proficiency in a subject area in order to earn college credit. Institutions, however, can use various combinations of CLEP exams to assess their general education program (such as English composition, social sciences and history, college mathematics, and natural sciences). Unlike the other assessment instruments discussed here, CLEP is completely geared toward assessing individuals; the publisher does not provide institutional-level data. A more elaborate discussion of CLEP appears in Chapter Five.

Collegiate Learning Assessment. Unlike other assessment instruments that focus on subject areas, the Collegiate Learning Assessment (CLA; http://www.cae.org/content/pro_collegiate.htm) is aimed at assessing students' higher-order thinking skills. Students are provided with a scenario and documents and asked to give written responses to tasks that evaluate and assess their critical thinking, analytical, problem-solving, and communication skills. (See the following link for an example: www.cae.org/content/pro_collegiate_sample_measures.htm.)

The CLA provides institution-level data to assist faculty, department chairs, and administrators in improving teaching and learning.

NEW DIRECTIONS FOR INSTITUTIONAL RESEARCH • DOI: 10.1002/ir

Defining Issues Test. The Center for the Study of Ethical Development at the University of Minnesota produces the Defining Issues Test (DIT; http://www.centerforthestudyofethicaldevelopment.net/Ordering%20DITs%20and%20Materials.htm), which evaluates a person's moral reasoning based on three schemas: personal interest, maintaining norms, and postconventional. The DIT-2, created in 1999, is shorter and more up-to-date, and it is slightly more powerful in producing validity trends. Both the DIT and DIT-2 take about forty-five to fifty minutes to complete, while a shorter DIT takes about thirty-five to forty minutes.

ETS Proficiency Profile. The Proficiency Profile (http://www.ets.org/portal/site/ets/menuitem.1488512ecfd5b8849a77b13bc3921509/?vgnextoid=ff3aaf5e44df4010VgnVCM10000022f95190RCRD&vgnextchannel=f98546f1674f4010VgnVCM10000022f95190RCRD), previously known as the Measure of Academic Proficiency and Progress, assesses students in four areas through multiple-choice questions: critical thinking, reading, writing, and mathematics. (See the following link for sample questions: http://www.ets.org/Media/Tests/MAPP/pdf/mappsampleques.pdf.)

The standard test takes two hours and has 108 questions, while the abbreviated form takes forty minutes and has 36 questions. Institutions have the option to add an essay question or up to fifty locally developed questions. ETS provides both norm-referenced (allows for group comparisons) and criterion-referenced scores (measures proficiencies of individual test takers). Comparative data are available, as over 380 institutions and 375,000 students have participated in the ETS Proficiency Profile.

Watson Glaser—Critical Thinking. The Watson Glazer (http://talentlens.com/en/assessments/watson_glaser.php) assesses individuals' critical thinking skills based on their ability to recognize assumptions, evaluate arguments, and draw conclusions. (See the following link for sample questions: http://talentlens.com/en/downloads/samplequestion/WatsonGlaser_Form_AB_Example_Questions.pdf.)

The standard form lasts forty to sixty minutes, and the short form lasts thirty to forty-five minutes. Data are provided at the individual level.

Purchasing an Assessment Management and Reporting System. Several vendors offer assessment management and reporting systems, and this is a viable option for many campuses. The best of these systems integrates student learning assessment into the mission, goals, and planning activities of the institution. All three of those listed here offer consulting and software targeted toward demonstrating and enhancing institutional effectiveness for accountability and accreditation, as well as establishing a culture of evidence-based continuous improvement. The student learning assessment component tends to focus on general education core competencies, which is why we refer to these in this chapter.

TaskStream (www.taskstream.com) offers a goal-driven accountability management system for demonstrating institutional effectiveness with learning achievement tools for assessing student performance. TaskStream serves secondary schools, institutions of higher education, and not-for-profits. Its performance reporting system for educational organizations is supported by curricular mapping, e-portfolios, and surveys of students, faculty, alumni, and employers. Its Web site does not list the institutions served.

Tk20 CampusWide (www.Tk20.com) offers an assessment and reporting system that is driven by locally articulated statements of mission, goals, objectives, and outcomes. The comprehensive reporting system integrates data from all campus sources and produces a series of dashboard reports for each measureable outcome. The software is customizable at the institution, college, department, or program levels, and is available in three configurations of capability and detail ranging from tested student learning, retention, and curricular mapping to course evaluations, faculty activity, e-portfolios, and student advisement. The Tk20 Web site lists approximately 100 colleges and universities that have used its services.

WeaveOnline (www.weaveonline.com) is a Web-based assessment and planning application that helps colleges and universities manage accreditation, assessment, and planning processes for quality assurance and enhancement. WeaveOnline aligns courses and student experiences with desired outcomes and accreditation standards. It was originally developed by a team of assessment and planning professionals at Virginia Commonwealth University and now lists over 150 member institutions, public and private, two-year and four-year. A strength of WeaveOnline is the sharing of successful practices with the other participating member institutions.

Conclusion

This chapter has summarized some of the most important considerations for evaluating student general education knowledge and skills, including the assessment process and available methodologies and instruments. The work of the AAC&U is a valuable resource for institutional researchers, administrators, and faculty members alike. We conclude with the following helpful tips for designing and executing an effective general education assessment plan (AAC&U, 2004b, p. 19). Effective plans contain these elements:

> The use of both formative assessment, for the purpose of giving feedback and making improvement, and summative assessment, for the purpose of identifying levels of attainment.
>
> Multiple methods that include both qualitative and quantitative evidence.
>
> Authentic methods that arise from students' actual assignments and learning experiences, which might be both curricular and cocurricular.
>
> Assessments that are developmental, so that students and others can observe progress toward valued outcomes, perhaps through the use of portfolios.

A focus on higher, more sophisticated knowledge and capacities rather than on more easily measured basic skills.

Faculty ownership of not just the education but also, because it is inherent to the learning process itself, the assessment of students. Whether they teach major or general education courses, faculty need to create, implement, and sustain the program to educate and assess students.

Assessments as continuous, systematic, and multidimensional.

An ongoing, systematic process for using assessments results to improve teaching, learning, and the curriculum.

Thus, the purpose of general education assessment is not only to evaluate a student's knowledge but also to provide feedback to improve the educational process for future students.

Finally, institutional researchers should not be afraid to examine the technologies available when designing any assessment project. The students of this generation entering school are often experts of the Internet, and institutional researchers should take advantage of the students' propensity to blog. Using Web technology like Blackboard, Course Management Systems, or WEBCAT can make some assessments more applicable. Institutional researchers should also investigate how new hardware technologies can improve assessment.

Appendix A: General Education

As discussed in this chapter, the AAC&U *Greater Expectations* national panel identified the skills needed to succeed in the twenty-first century by "intentional learners" (AAC&U, 2002, pp. 22–24). The intentional learner is empowered through intellectual and practical skills that include:

- Communicating in diverse settings and groups, using written, oral, and visual means, and in more than one language
- Understanding and employing both quantitative and qualitative analysis to describe and solve problems
- Interpreting, evaluating, and using information discerningly from a variety of sources
- Integrating knowledge of various types and understanding complex systems
- Resolving difficult issues creatively by employing multiple systems and tools
- Deriving meaning from experience, as well as gathering information from observation
- Demonstrating intellectual agility and managing change
- Transforming information into knowledge and knowledge into judgment and action

- Working well in teams, including those of diverse composition, and building consensus

The intentional learner is informed by knowledge and ways of knowing. The student learns:

- The human imagination, expression, and the products of many cultures
- The interrelations within and among global and cross-cultural communities
- Means of modeling the natural, social, and technical worlds
- The values and histories underlying U.S. democracy

The intentional learner is responsible for personal actions and civic values. Education should develop a student's:

- Intellectual honesty and engagement in ongoing learning
- Responsibility for society's moral health and for social justice
- Active participation as a citizen of a diverse democracy
- Respect for and appropriate use of intuition and feeling, as well as thinking
- Discernment of consequences, including ethical consequences, of decisions and actions
- Deep understanding of one's self and one's multiple identities that connect habits of mind, heart, and body
- Respect for the complex identities of others, their histories, and their cultures

Appendix B: Advantages and Disadvantages of Various Assessment Strategies

Advantages and Disadvantages of Most Commercially Published Standardized Exams

Advantages
- Can be implemented quickly with minimal faculty and staff time.
- Reduces or eliminates faculty workload for instrument development and scoring.
- Offers objective scoring (especially for multiple-choice items).
- Comparative data and norms usually available.
- Validity and reliability established through content specification, expert panel reviews, and pilot testing.
- Short turnaround time for results.
- Professional help usually available.
- Usually more legitimacy of results with stakeholders.

Disadvantages
- The test may or may not be congruent with campus-specific general education goals.

NEW DIRECTIONS FOR INSTITUTIONAL RESEARCH • DOI: 10.1002/ir

- The test may bypass the important process of clarifying learning goals and objectives typically associated with local testing development.
- The test may be costly in dollars rather than time.
- Some instruments produce norm-referenced results that tend to be less meaningful than criterion-referenced results.
- Norm-referenced data are dependent on the institutions in the comparison groups and methods of selecting students to be tested in those institutions.
- Group-administered multiple-choice tests can have a potentially high degree of error.
- The test usually provides summative data only (no formative evaluation).

Locally Developed Exams (Including Essays)

Advantages
- Content and style can be geared to specific goals, objectives, and student characteristics of the institution or program.
- Specific criteria for performance can be established in relationship to the curriculum.
- The process of development can lead to clarification of what is important in the process and content of student learning.
- Local grading by faculty can provide immediate feedback and be an excellent faculty development activity, especially if faculty from a variety of disciplines are included.
- There may be greater faculty and institutional control over the interpretation and use of results.
- Formative assessment for program improvement is more likely.

Disadvantages
- Require considerable leadership and coordination, especially during the various phases of development.
- Costly in terms of time and effort (more front-load effort for objective test; more back-load effort for essays).
- Demand expertise in measurement to ensure validity, reliability, and utility.
- Results may have less legitimacy with stakeholders.

Simulation or Performance Appraisals

Advantages
- Provide a more direct measure of what has been learned.
- Preferable to most other methods in measuring the application and generalization of learning.
- Practical application likely to be more relevant to students than tests or essays.

- Better means of evaluating depth and breadth of student skill development than multiple-choice tests or other nonperformance-based measures.
- Very flexible; some degree of simulation can be arranged for virtually any discipline or student target skill.
- For many skills, simulations can be group administered, thus providing an excellent combination of quality and economy.
- Process of development and grading likely to provide faculty dialogue and development.
- Particularly relevant to goals and objectives of professional training programs and disciplines with well-defined skill development.

Disadvantages
- Ratings and grading typically more subjective than standardized tests.
- Requires considerable time and effort to establish and apply grading criteria.
- More expensive than traditional testing option.

Surveys and Questionnaires

Advantages
- Content flexibility and ease of instrument construction, especially with survey software.
- Assesses the perspective that students, alumni, or others have of the institution, which may lead to beneficial changes to relationships with these groups.
- Conveys a sense of importance regarding the opinions of constituent groups.
- Ease of response often reaches individuals who otherwise might be missing from assessment efforts.
- Results easily understood and typically do not require expert interpretation.
- Relatively inexpensive to design and administer, allowing larger sample sizes.

Disadvantages
- Results tend to be highly dependent on wording of items, salience of survey, and organization of instrument. Thus, good surveys and questionnaires are more difficult to construct than they appear.
- Frequently rely on volunteer responses, which may not be representative.
- Mail surveys tend to yield low response rates.
- Forced-response choice may not allow respondents to express their true opinions.
- Results reflect perceptions, attitudes, or behaviors that individuals are willing to report and thus consist of indirect evidence that may have less legitimacy with stakeholders.

- Research suggests that such data are better for measuring and comparing the responses of groups rather than individuals.

Interviews and Focus Groups

Advantages
- Interviews tend to have most of the attributes of surveys and questionnaires with flexibility of content and ease of construction.
- Allow for more individualized questions and follow-up probes based on the responses of interviewees.
- Provide immediate feedback.
- Frequently yield benefits beyond data collection that come from opportunities to interact with students and other groups.
- Can include a greater variety of items than is possible on surveys and questionnaires, including those that provide more direct measures of learning and development.

Disadvantages
- Require direct contact, which may be difficult to arrange, require special approval, and limit accessibility to certain populations, and may raise concerns regarding protection of rights and confidentiality.
- May be intimidating to the interviewees, thus altering their responses.
- Results tend to be highly dependent on wording of items and the manner in which interviews are conducted.
- Time-consuming and labor intensive compared to most other methods, thus producing smaller sample sizes.

External Examiners

Advantages
- Increase impartiality, third-party objectivity (external validity).
- Feedback useful for both student and program evaluation.
- Provide opportunities for valuable program consultations.
- May serve to stimulate other collaborative efforts between departments or institutions.

Disadvantages
- Always some risk of a misfit between examiners' expertise or the expectations and program outcomes.
- Logistics may be difficult to arrange, particularly when making arrangements with a teaching faculty member.
- For individualized evaluations or large programs, can be costly and time-consuming.

Archival Records and Transcript Analysis

Advantages
- Analyze information and events that have already occurred.
- Tend to be readily available, thus requiring little additional effort.
- Constitute unobtrusive measurement, not requiring additional time or effort from student or other groups.
- Can be very useful for longitudinal studies.
- Cost-efficient.

Disadvantages
- Especially in large institutions, may require considerable effort and coordination to determine exactly what data are available.
- If individual records are included, may raise concerns regarding protection of rights and confidentiality.
- May encourage finding ways to use the data rather than finding ways to measure specific goals and objectives.
- Historical views of what happened may not reflect what is happening now or why it is happening.

Portfolios

Advantages
- Can be used to view learning and development longitudinally and in depth, a valid and useful perspective.
- Multiple components of a curriculum can be measured at the same time.
- Samples in a portfolio are more likely than test results to reflect student ability when preplanning, input from others, and similar opportunities common to most work settings are available.
- The process of reviewing and grading portfolios provides an excellent opportunity for faculty exchange and development, discussion of curriculum goals and objectives, review of grading criteria, and program feedback.
- Greater faculty control over interpretation and use of results.
- Economical in terms of student time and effort, since no separate assessment administration time is required.
- Results are more likely to be meaningful at all levels and can be used for diagnostic and prescriptive purposes as well.
- Avoid or minimize test anxiety and other one-shot measurement problems.
- Increase power of maximum performance measures over more artificial or restrictive speed measures on test or in-class sample.

Disadvantages
- Costly in terms of evaluator time and effort.
- Management of the collection and grading process, including the establishment of reliable and valid grading criteria, is likely to be challenging.

- May not provide external legitimacy.
- If samples to be included have been previously submitted for course grades, faculty may be concerned that a hidden agenda of the process is to validate their grading.
- Security concerns may arise as to whether submitted samples are the students' own work or adhere to other measurement criteria.

Behavioral Observations

Advantages

- Particularly suited to assessing goals pertaining to attitudes, values, and behaviors.
- Best way to evaluate degree to which attitudes and values are put into action.
- Catching students being themselves is the most natural form of assessment.
- Least intrusive assessment option, since the purpose is to avoid any interference with typical student activities.

Disadvantages

- Always some risk of confounded results due to the observer effect (subjects may behave atypically if they know they are being observed).
- Depending on the target behavior, there may be socially or professionally sensitive issues to be dealt with or even legal considerations.
- May encourage "big brother" perception of assessment or institution, or both.
- Inexperienced or inefficient observers can produce unreliable, invalid results.

Student Self-Evaluation

Advantages

- Encourage active participation of students in their own learning and development.
- May encourage more faculty-student collaboration and dialogue.
- If feedback is provided, may prompt greater student awareness of the types of criteria faculty use to evaluate work in college and how those compare to students' own standards.
- Time and effort devoted to the process are more likely than some other methods to prompt individual learning and development.
- Self-reflection and self-evaluation are important skills for lifelong learning.
- Low cost.

Disadvantages

- The use of potentially different criteria for different students reduces reliability and the ability to generalize results across students, settings, and years.

- Self-evaluation is among the most subjective methods of assessment.
- Relationships between self-evaluations and more traditional measures may be quite tenuous.
- Research has suggested that students in the United States may be particularly prone to expressing self-confidence in their own academic abilities despite evidence to the contrary.
- Better for measuring and comparing the responses of groups rather than individuals.
- Best if supplemented by other assessment information.

Classroom Research

Advantages
- Provides direct feedback to faculty, enabling them to adjust instruction quickly.
- Encourages teachers to make goals and objectives explicit and to use assessment techniques that address such goals and objectives.
- Encourages multimethod approaches to assessment.
- Provides direct links between the teaching-learning process and outcomes.
- Tends to be a powerful vehicle for faculty development.

Disadvantages
- Results typically are based on small sample sizes with few controls for differences in student backgrounds.
- Faculty may lack the needed skills in research methods and statistics.
- May be difficult to replicate and generalize the results to other classrooms, curricula, and policies.
- Research at the classroom level may be difficult to aggregate for institutional assessment purposes.

References

Association of American Colleges and Universities. *Greater Expectations: A New Vision for Learning as a Nation Goes to College.* Washington, DC: Author, 2002.

Association of American Colleges and Universities. *Taking Responsibility for the Quality of the Baccalaureate Degree.* Washington, DC: Author, 2004a.

Association of American Colleges and Universities. *Our Students' Best Work: A Framework for Accountability Worthy of our Mission.* Washington, DC: Author, 2004b.

Association of American Colleges and Universities. *Liberal Education Outcomes: A Preliminary Report on Student Achievement in College.* Washington, DC: Author, 2005.

Bauer, K. "Assessment in institutional research." In W. E. Knight (ed.), *The primer for institutional research.* Tallahassee, FL: Association for Institutional Research, 2003.

Boyer, E. L., and Levine, A. *A Quest for Common Learning: The Aims of General Education.* Washington, DC: The Carnegie Foundation for the Advancement of Teaching, 1981.

Friedman, T. *The World Is Flat: A Brief History of the Twenty-First Century.* New York: Farrar, Straus, and Giroux, 2006.

Lattuca, L. R., and Stark, J. S. *Shaping the College Curriculum: Academic Plans in Context.* Needham Heights, MA: Allyn & Bacon, 2009.

Middle States Commission on Higher Education. *Characteristics of Excellence in Higher Education: Eligibility Requirements and Standards for Accreditation* (12th ed.) Philadelphia: Author, 2006.

New England Association of Schools and Colleges, Commission on Institutions of Higher Education. *Standards for Accreditation.* Bedford, MA: Author, 2005. Retrieved February 6, 2010, from http://cihe.neasc.org/standards_policies/standards/standards_html_version.

North Central Association of Colleges and Schools, Higher Learning Commission. *Handbook of Accreditation.* (3rd ed.) Chicago: Author, 2003. Retrieved February 6, 2010, from http://www.nwccu.org/Pubs%20Forms%20and%20Updates/Publications/Accreditation%20Handbook.pdf.

Northwest Commission on Colleges and Universities. *Accreditation Handbook.* Redmond, WA: Author, 2003. Retrieved February 2, 2010, from http://www.nwccu.org/Pubs%20Forms%20and%20Updates/Publications/Accreditation%20Handbook.pdf.

Ratcliff, J. L., Johnson, D. K., La Nasa, S. M., and Gaff, J. G. *The Status of General Education in the Year 2000: Summary of National Survey.* Washington, DC: Association of American Colleges and Universities, 2001.

Southern Association of Colleges and Schools, Commission on Colleges. *Principles of Accreditation: Foundations for Quality Enhancement.* Decatur, GA: Author, 2008. Retrieved February 6, 2010, from http://www.sacscoc.org/pdf/2008Principlesof Accreditation.pdf.

Stark, J., and Lowther, M. *Strengthening the Ties that Bind: Integrating Undergraduate Liberal and Professional Study.* Ann Arbor: Professional Preparation Network, University of Michigan, 1988.

Tebo-Messina, M., and Prus, J. "Assessing general education: An overview of methods." Paper presented at the American Association for Higher Education 10th Annual Conference on Assessment and Quality, Boston, June 11–14, 1995.

Volkwein, J. F. "Assessing Institutional Effectiveness and Connecting the Pieces of a Fragmented University." In J. Burke (ed.), *Fixing the Fragmented University.* San Francisco: Jossey-Bass/Anker, 2007.

Volkwein, J. F. "AIR Assessment Workshop." Presented at the Annual Meeting of AIR in Atlanta, May 2009.

Volkwein, J. F., and Bauer, K. W. "The Roles and Uses of Institutional Research in Decision Making and Assessment." Workshop presented at the Department of Defense Conference on Civilian Education and Professional Development, Fort Lesley McNair, Washington, D.C., 2002.

Western Association of Schools and Colleges. *WASC Handbook of Accreditation.* Alameda, CA: Author, 2008. Retrieved February 6, 2010, from http://www.wascsenior.org/findit/files/forms/Handbook_of_Accreditation_2008_with_hyperlinks.pdf.

Recommended Reading

Association of American Colleges and Universities. *Strong Foundations: Twelve Principles for Effective General Education Programs.* Washington, DC: Author, 1994.

Middle States Commission on Higher Education. *Student Learning Assessment: Options and Resources.* (2nd ed.) Philadelphia: Author, 2007.

Osterlind, S. J. *A National Review of Scholastic Achievement in General Education: How Are We Doing and Why Should We Care?* ASHE-ERIC Higher Education Report, vol. 25, no. 8. Washington, DC: The George Washington University, Graduate School of Education and Human Development, 1997.

ALEXANDER C. YIN *is a senior project associate of the Center for the Study of Higher Education at The Pennsylvania State University.*

J. FREDERICKS VOLKWEIN *is emeritus professor of higher education at The Pennsylvania State University and a former director of the Center for the Study of Higher Education.*

7

This chapter summarizes the diverse assessment methods and strategies for measuring student academic attainment and describes the key elements in one university's assessment implementation.

Assessing Student Learning in the Major Field of Study

J. Fredericks Volkwein

Assessing student attainment in the major field of study is increasingly important to employers and accrediting bodies alike. Construction and manufacturing firms do not like engineers who design faulty bridges and airplanes. Marketing firms want to hire students who understand the difference between a niche market and a global market. School districts want teachers who understand the different levels of Bloom's taxonomy in order to adapt their teaching technique to student learning styles. Graduate schools want students who are knowledgeable in their field. Moreover, practitioners in many fields not only need a degree from an accredited program, but also need to pass a licensure exam or undergo individual certification (such as in accounting, architecture, civil engineering, law, medicine, nursing, social work, and teaching). This chapter outlines the foundations for assessing student learning in the major, summarizes the instruments and strategies used for assessing these outcomes, and discusses some important considerations in the process.

While identifying the separate assessment domains (basic skills, general education, attainment in the major field of study, and student personal development), we need to understand how fluid the boundaries are among them—how, in fact, each institution creates an educationally interdependent environment. For example, student attainment of basic reading and writing and mathematics skills directly supports student performance in

New Directions for Institutional Research, Assessment Supplement 2009, Spring 2010 © Wiley Periodicals, Inc.
Published online in Wiley InterScience (www.interscience.wiley.com) • DOI: 10.1002/ir.333

general education and in the major. The educational breadth of a general education program and the intellectual depth of the major are mutually reinforcing. Moreover, students must assume personal responsibility for their own growth in order to meet their responsibilities to the faculty. One's intellectual development cannot be easily separated from one's personal and social development, nor can liberal learning and disciplinary expertise be completely independent of each other.

Nevertheless, institutions usually choose different paths. Congruent with their separate missions, community college staff usually concentrate more heavily on basic skills assessment, faculty at private liberal arts colleges often devote greater attention to general education assessment, and faculty at research universities and in professional disciplines are much more interested in assessing student attainment in the major and graduate programs. The larger and more fragmented multiversities usually find it difficult to galvanize faculty efforts in basic skills, general education, and noncognitive development, but faculty in nearly all institutions can see the benefits of examining student attainment in the major concentration. This chapter focuses on assisting faculty with strategies for assessing student attainment in the major field of study.

Previous chapters in this volume have referred to some of the key questions for assessing student learning:

- What should students learn, and what ways do we expect them to grow? These are questions about goals and the answers require goal clarity.
- What do students learn, and in what ways do they actually grow? These are measurement questions, and the answer requires measureable evidence of learning and growth.
- What should we do to facilitate and enhance student learning and growth? This question about educational improvement requires effective use of assessment results.

Thus, the goals question and the improvement question are both strongly linked to the challenges of measurement and implementation. We recognized this reality in Chapter Two, which discusses the institutional effectiveness model. Campus assessment programs need to speak to both the inspirational and the pragmatic, the simultaneous needs for internal improvement and external accountability. Moreover, these generic assessment questions drive research design and data collection:

- Do we meet the standards?
- How do we compare?
- Are we meeting our goals?
- Are we getting better?
- Are our efforts productive?

Methods for Assessing Student Attainment in the Major

At universities with well-developed strategies for assessment in the major, each department constructs an appropriate means for assessing student attainment using a broad range of possible assessment designs. In some departments where the numbers of majors are small, the faculty might focus on the achievement of all students. Other departments, perhaps with large numbers of majors, may decide to study representative groups of students. The aim of the assessment is not to magnify any particular student's success or failure but rather to judge, in whatever ways we can, students' abilities to construct knowledge for themselves and assess the work of faculty in nurturing, enhancing, and enabling those abilities. Departments might combine some of the elements discussed in this chapter or might design a unique approach not considered here. The objectives are to examine what it is students are acquiring when they major in a particular discipline and to use that information to enhance the learning experience for future students. The assessment strategies listed here each have advantages and disadvantages, some of which are outlined in Chapter Six, Appendix B.

Comprehensive Exams. Comprehensive exams can be locally or commercially designed. When such exams are designed locally by the faculty, they have the advantage of being shaped to fit the department's curriculum. Departmental exams have the disadvantages of needing labor-intensive annual revision and local scoring by the faculty and lack a comparison group. Commercially designed standardized instruments provide scoring services and more reliable and valid comparison groups, but they may or may not fit the department's curriculum and are not useful in disciplines wishing to go beyond a multiple-choice format.

Some departments have attempted to use the Graduate Record Examination (GRE) score in the discipline as an assessment tool, even though it is generally not appropriate for this purpose. GRE scores have several deficiencies as assessment tools. First, the scores are relational and answer only the question, "How do you compare?" You do not know what a score of 600 means in terms of student achievement because you do not know how many questions were answered correctly and incorrectly. Second, it uses the wrong comparison group. Instead of comparing each GRE score against those of all college graduates, student GRE scores are in relation to a graduate school–bound population. Third, there are no GRE subfield scores within each major field, so you cannot tell if student performance is congruent with the student's curriculum.

The ETS Major Field Exam was constructed in response to these weaknesses in the GRE. The exam scores not only are normed on populations of graduating seniors and not only indicate the number answered correct (nonrelational), but also report scores by subfield, thus providing useful information for analyzing the curriculum.

New Directions for Institutional Research • DOI: 10.1002/ir

Senior Thesis or Research Project. Such a requirement encourages students to use the tools of the discipline on a focused task as the culmination of their undergraduate academic experience. Under ideal conditions, each department or program uses the student's work to reflect on what students are achieving with the aim of evaluating, and if necessary strengthening, the curriculum and experiences of students within that major.

Performance or Fieldwork Experience. Asking students to demonstrate in some practical or even public way the knowledge and skills they have learned and acquired, this emphasizes the integration and application of the separate facets of the academic major. Such a requirement may be especially fitting in professional fields like social work and teaching, as well as in performing arts fields. Examples include student recitals, art exhibitions, practice teaching, and supervised field experiences.

Capstone Course. This is usually a required senior course designed to integrate the study of the discipline. It often has a heavy research and writing component. Such courses offer ideal opportunities to assess student learning and strengthen the curriculum of that major. Often the course can contain some other form of assessment, such as a local or national exam, embedded within it.

Student Portfolio of Learning Experiences. In this mode of assessment, students collect systematically the work that they have undertaken in their study of a discipline. They undertake and write a self-examination of the material, demonstrating how they have constructed the discipline through their writing and thinking over two years of study. Afterward faculty meet with students to go over this portfolio. The faculty then could use their own and the students' analyses of portfolios, coupled with their perceptions of the student conferences, as a basis for conversation among faculty about the curriculum and practices within a discipline. In departments selecting this option, all faculty responsible for undergraduate education should be part of this process, but the plan becomes difficult to implement if each faculty member has to assess overly large numbers of students.

Senior Essay and Interview. The faculty constructs a series of questions that ask students to demonstrate their conceptual understanding of the discipline and reflect on the strengths and weaknesses of their programs. The students respond in writing and then meet with faculty to discuss their written statements. The faculty next meet to discuss the results of their conferences with students for the purpose of strengthening the major. Large departments may sample a cross-section of seniors rather than the entire population.

New Directions for Institutional Research • DOI: 10.1002/ir

Other Suggestions. Academic departments and programs have other options as well.

- Academic departments have other options as well: Course-embedded assessment, for example, a standardized examination, a classroom research project, or a comparison of a written assignment at the beginning of the course and one at the end
- Student self-assessment, for example, of a written exercise or after viewing a video of his or her performance or presentation
- Student peer assessment, which also builds a learning culture in the department
- Secondary reading of a student's regular course work by faculty colleagues (this requires an atmosphere of department collegiality)
- External examiners or readers, which puts the student and faculty member on the same learning team
- Using historical department data on student performance and placement and course-taking patterns (these are discussed more thoroughly in Chapters 8, 9, and 10)
- Faculty focus group discussions with students
- Surveys of students and alumni using self-reported measures

Table 7.1 gives a summary of possible methods for assessing student attainment in the major depending on each purpose. The suggestions contained in the table should be treated as guides for departmental consideration rather than as definitive uses. A capstone course or departmental exam might be the most useful choice for assessing the student's attainment of faculty-determined performance standards. For the purposes of meeting professional or national standards, a standardized test or external examiner may be employed. Comparing a student's performance to some external reference group almost always requires the use of a national exam or performance standard, but even graduate school and placement information can be used for comparative purposes. Measuring the attainment of educational goals requires student-centered strategies such as learning portfolios, focus groups, or locally designed exams. To answer the improvement question, a wide range of strategies using multiple sources of information can be used to examine trends over time.

Many professional organizations in the disciplines have developed exams, such as the Fundamentals of Engineering Exam, the Business Management Test, the American Chemical Society Exam, the ETS PRAXIS tests for beginning teachers, and the National Teacher Education tests in professional knowledge and in various specialties. Many states and specialized accrediting bodies require exam passage as a condition for professional licensure, especially in the medical and health professions, accounting, law, civil engineering, and architecture. In such cases, faculty usually shape the

Table 7.1. Assessment in the Undergraduate Major Field of Study

Purposes	Suggested Strategies and Methods
Meeting standards	Department comprehensive exam Capstone course with embedded assessment Senior thesis or research project External examiners or readers Student performance or exhibit with expert judgments Practice teaching, internships, fieldwork Proficiency or competency tests Certification exams
Comparing to others	National comprehensive exams (ETS major field, College Level Examination Program, ACT) Discipline-based exams Peer assessments Program review by external experts Comparative graduate school and placement information
Measuring goal attainment	Senior thesis and research project Student portfolio Student self-assessment Faculty or student focus groups Alumni surveys Exhibits, performances, internships, field experiences Capstone course with embedded assessment Locally designed tests of competency/proficiency
Developing talent and program improvement	All of the above, especially: Senior essay followed by faculty interview Faculty-student focus groups Course-embedded assessment Learning portfolio Alumni surveys Analysis of historical, archival, or transcript data Self-reported growth

curriculum to maximize student performance. Other tests have been developed by national testing companies, such as the ETS Major Field Achievement Tests and GRE Subject Tests, the College Level Examination Program Subject Exams, and ACT Proficiency Exams. In addition, to evaluate student attainment in the major, many institutions rely on locally designed exams, course-embedded assessments, performance or field experiences, capstone experiences, and self-reported mastery on dimensions that are locally constructed.

Collecting and Sharing Data

Each assessment question or purpose can be addressed in a variety of appropriate ways. The question of whether the activity is relatively centralized

NEW DIRECTIONS FOR INSTITUTIONAL RESEARCH • DOI: 10.1002/ir

and controlled by forces outside the department, or decentralized and controlled by the faculty, is perhaps less important than the usefulness of the assessment for enhancing student learning. Even nationally normed standardized tests can be used by faculty locally to reflect on the strengths and weaknesses of the department's program. And even the most locally-centered form of student assessment usually yields results that over time can be aggregated to serve program evaluation and institutional accountability purposes.

There are many appropriate uses and efficiencies to be gained from relatively centralized data collection activities carried out in campus offices of institutional research. Institutional researchers often work with others on the campus to develop and maintain student and alumni information systems that can serve as rich assessment databases. Rather than developing their own survey research, database, and software expertise, departments can draw on these centralized databases in conducting their own assessment activities.

A healthy assessment culture is created when cooperative data sharing occurs between administrative offices and academic departments. In recent years, a variety of campuses have downloaded from their centrally maintained student and alumni databases a variety of information that is helpful to student and program assessment by faculty. The cost to the institution of conducting separate alumni surveys in each department and maintaining independent databases is too high. By surveying several thousand alumni, campuses can distribute both aggregated and disaggregated summaries on a wide range of measures of alumni satisfaction, educational outcomes, intellectual growth, career development, and effectiveness of the undergraduate experience, both departmental and campuswide.

A Case Study: How One University Responded

Over the past two decades, many universities have created assessment blue-ribbon committees, panels, task forces, and planning teams. Such efforts produce the most enduring results when there is both administrative support and faculty ownership. At one university, the assessment committee report recommended that each academic department construct a means for collecting information about student attainment in the undergraduate major as an integral part of a comprehensive plan of departmental self-study and development. They viewed assessing student attainment in the major as part of larger curricular review, program evaluation, and development efforts by the faculty.

The assessment committee concluded that student grades in specific courses constitute necessary but not sufficient information about student attainment. Indeed, some faculty give grades based on students' reaching a standard of proficiency and knowledge; some grade on the curve; some grade student performance on the attainment of learning goals and objectives embedded in the course; and some grade on the basis of student effort and improvement. What was needed was a more comprehensive view of student achievement in each discipline. In this context, student grades, faculty teaching evaluations, periodic program reviews, alumni studies, and student test scores all constitute complementary ways of obtaining useful feedback in order to improve learning in the major.

In its plan, the assessment committee and the provost recommended a menu of departmental assessment choices and encouraged departments to design their own if they wished. Most departments submitted plans for assessment in the major, and after review and evaluation, some departments began implementation, while others clearly needed assistance in the form of assessment workshops.

Departmental proposals covered a wide range of assessment strategies, including standardized tests, senior research and writing projects, course-embedded examinations, capstone courses, student performances and field-work, and student portfolios and essays. For a more detailed list of assessment strategies elected by each department, see Volkwein (2004). Tailored to suit the needs of each discipline, these efforts gave the university, and especially the faculty, a rich array of information for improving the learning experience of undergraduate students. One key to the program's success was the provost's demand that every department try at least one assessment method and see what it learned from it.

After a year or two of experience with one form of assessment, many departments explored another form of assessment, thus adding to the richness of the faculty's collective understanding about the effectiveness of the curriculum. One form of assessment evidence sheds light on meeting standards, while another reflected student growth or program improvement. One strategy enabled peer comparisons, while another yielded evidence of goal attainment. Judgments of student learning and program effectiveness will be better and richer if they are based on multiple indicators and measures, and they will be less reliable if based on a single indicator or measure. A multidimensional approach yields a far more reliable image of strengths and weaknesses. For example, when a department sees congruence between the information it receives from graduating seniors' test results and from alumni survey results, it has more confidence in the strength of the findings.

Consistent with the assessment committee recommendations, most campus efforts reflected a commitment to ongoing self-reflective development. Departmental plans, with few exceptions, reflected a willingness to begin assessment and learn from it—to integrate assessment into the department's self-reflective improvement. In a few cases, departments were skeptical and unwilling to undertake assessment in the absence of perfect measures and methodologies. Successful assessment programs on other campuses suggest that perfection is unattainable and that there is much to be learned from getting started, building on the familiar, and developing more informative and effective strategies based on experience over time.

NEW DIRECTIONS FOR INSTITUTIONAL RESEARCH • DOI: 10.1002/ir

Conclusion

An important ingredient in a successful assessment program is an attitude of cooperation and trust among faculty and between faculty and administrative staff (Terenzini, 1989). Faculty need to be trusted to use the information for the enhancement of student learning, and administrators need to be trusted to use the summary information to promote institutional effectiveness. Obviously assessment evidence has the power to change faculty behavior, but it should not be used for faculty evaluation. The goal of collecting assessment information should be to promote evidenced-based thinking and new conversations about student learning and about the curricular experiences that promote student learning. Ideally the faculty rewards structure should be shaped to reward constructive changes rather than to punish poor performance.

References

Terenzini, P. T. "Assessment with Open Eyes: Pitfalls in Studying Student Outcomes. *Journal of Higher Education*, 1989, 60, 644–664.

Volkwein, J. F. "Assessing Student Learning in the Major: What's the Question?" In B. Keith (ed.), *Contexts for learning: Institutional strategies for managing curricular change through assessment*. Stillwater, OK: New Forums Press, 2004.

Recommended Reading

Applebaum, M. I. "Assessment Through the Major." In C. Adelman (ed.), *Performance and Judgment: Essays on the Principles and Practice in the Assessment of College Student Learning*. Washington, DC: U.S. Department of Education, 1989.

Banta, T. W., Lund, J. P., Black, K. E., and Oblander, F. W. (eds). "Assessing Student Achievement in the Major." In *Assessment in Practice: Putting Principles to Work on College Campuses*. San Francisco: Jossey-Bass, 1996.

Ratcliff, J. L. "What Can We Learn from Coursework Patterns About Improving the Undergraduate Curriculum?" In J. L. Ratcliff (ed.), *Assessment and Curriculum*. New Directions for Higher Education, no. 80. San Francisco: Jossey-Bass, 1992.

Suskie, L. *Assessing Student Learning: A Common Sense Guide*. (2nd ed.) San Francisco: Jossey-Bass, 2009.

Walvoord, B. E. *Assessment Clear and Simple: A Practical Guide for Institutions, Departments and General Education*. San Francisco: Jossey-Bass, 2004.

J. Fredericks Volkwein *is emeritus professor of higher education at The Pennsylvania State University and a former director of the Center for the Study of Higher Education.*

New Directions for Institutional Research • DOI: 10.1002/ir

8

*This chapter summarizes the dominant student develop-
ment theories, notes important noncognitive outcomes,
and reviews several assessment instruments that measure
student personal growth.*

Assessing Personal Growth

Ying (Jessie) Liu, Alexander C. Yin

Chapters Two and Three address the power of using conceptual frameworks
and models to guide us in assessment design. We begin this chapter by
revisiting Astin, Panos, and Creager (1967), who developed a conceptual
scheme to guide the selection of various types of measurements organized
by three dimensions: type of outcome, type of data, and time. In assessing
basic skills, general education, and attainment of the major (the topics of
Chapters Five through Seven), the focus is on cognitive outcomes. In this
chapter, we look at affective or noncognitive outcomes (shown in left column of Table 8.1).

The theories and developmental stages discussed in this volume do not
occur just in college. Students' progress in their development at different
paces and much development continues after college as they encounter new
experiences and avenues for growth. Also, development happens for all individuals, not just college students. However, the research evidence suggests
that college experiences, as well as intentional programmatic efforts, may
cause college students to develop at more rapid rates than those who do not
attend college.

We thank the following on-line students for their contributions to our thinking for this
chapter: Sara Maene (Shepherd University), Nora Galambos (Stony Brook University),
James Mulik (College of the Marshall Islands), Eleanor Swanson (Monmouth University), and David Perez (Penn State University).

Table 8.1. Classification of Student Outcomes
by Type of Outcome and Type of Data

	Outcome	
Data	Affective	Cognitive
Psychological	Attitudes and values	Basic skills
	Educational and career goals	General education and critical thinking skills
	Satisfaction	Knowledge in the major
	Personal and social growth	Intellectual growth, academic performance (grade point average)
Behavioral	Choice of major	Educational attainment
	Choice of career	Occupational attainment
	Student-body leadership	
	Community leadership	

Why Institutional Researchers Should Care About Student Personal Growth

From *The American Freshman: National Norms for Fall 2004*, 74.6 percent of the survey participants noted career training as a very important reason for attending college. Higher education institutions try to accommodate this demand by teaching students as much content information as possible. Of course, we worry whether the students are developing cognitively, which is one reason that we assess students on basics skills, general education, and the major field. Yet higher education institutions cannot consider students to be empty computers enrolled in school just to gain the latest knowledge on the market.

Another important role of colleges and universities is developing a student's affective or noncognitive abilities. Reflect back to your days as an undergraduate student, and write down the most important lessons you learned in college. How many of these were cognitive, and how many were affective? No doubt, institutions should supply academic content material to students, because it would be irresponsible for schools to have students graduate academically unprepared. However, in life beyond the college years, it seems equally important for students to develop interpersonal skills. As globalization has made the world more connected, new graduates will be competing not just with people at the local or national level, but also with people globally. As more manufacturing and labor-intensive jobs become outsourced or automated and many more careers become service oriented, students who developed relational skills will be desired.

As institutional researchers, why should we care about personal and social growth? Banta, Lund, Black, and Oblander (1996) note that many institutions have an element of personal growth in their mission statements. Following are relevant portions of mission statements from several universities:

> The University of Arkansas Community College at Hope is an accredited, open-access, two-year institution of higher education committed to providing quality academic, occupational, personal growth, and cultural programs to support individual student and community needs in the Southwest Arkansas area.—University of Arkansas Community College at Hope

> The College aims to graduate women and men who can think clearly, who can speak and write persuasively and even eloquently, who can evaluate critically both their own and others' ideas, who can acquire new knowledge, and who are prepared in life and work to use their knowledge and their abilities to serve the common good.—Grinnell College

> Harvard seeks to identify and to remove restraints on students' full participation, so that individuals may explore their capabilities and interests and may develop their full intellectual and human potential. Education at Harvard should liberate students to explore, to create, to challenge, and to lead. The support the College provides to students is a foundation upon which self-reliance and habits of lifelong learning are built: Harvard expects that the scholarship and collegiality it fosters in its students will lead them in their later lives to advance knowledge, to promote understanding, and to serve society.—Harvard College

> In both undergraduate and graduate programs, experiential learning in the world of career and professional practice such as internships, field experiences, service learning, study abroad programs and other practical learning partnerships allow students to become directly involved in testing and applying academic theories and ongoing personal and professional development.—Plymouth State University

Most accrediting agency standards examine the congruence between the institution's mission statement and its accomplishments. Student development occupies a prominent place in most educational missions, so it is important to develop assessment processes that measure student cognitive and noncognitive development alike.

Yanikoski (2004) provides the following list of reasons that higher education leaders should assess character outcomes, which is an aspect of personal and social development:

- Character outcomes affect accreditation.
- Character outcomes can help recruit students.
- Character outcomes can increase philanthropy.
- Character outcomes captivate legislators.
- Character outcomes make graduates more successful in business.

- Character outcomes can transform campus life.
- Character outcomes confer bragging rights.
- Character outcomes can improve relations between the president and the board.
- Character outcomes improve society.

A Brief Primer on Psychosocial Development

Psychosocial development deals with how the individual relates to others and society and how the individual views the self. The concept of self includes identity and ego development, academic and social self-concept, and self-esteem. Relational development focuses on ways of interpreting and interacting with the rest of the world: with peers, authority figures, and significant others. Relational development encompasses such concepts as autonomy, locus of control, and independence; authoritarianism, dogmatism, and ethnocentrism; interpersonal relations; personal adjustment and psychological well-being; and maturity and general development.

Psychosocial developmental theories share many of the same attributes and assumptions:

- Development occurs in series, stages, or tasks when biology and psychology converge in an age-linked sequence, influenced by culture, society, and gender.
- Development consists of qualitative personal and interpersonal change related to thoughts, feelings, behaviors, values, and relationships.
- Development grows from the interaction between the person and the environment.
- Disequilibrium, dissonance, and anxiety force an individual to address an issue.
- Development benefits from regression and readdressing of previous failures and personal challenges.

Major Theorists. Psychosocial development theories for college students and young adults come out of Erik Erikson's work on development in the mid-1900s. The major theorists in psychosocial and identity development pertaining to college students are:

- Chickering (1969) and Chickering and Reisser (1993) on general identity development
- Josselson (1987) on women's identity development
- Cross (1995), Phinney (1990), and Helms (1995) on racial/ethnic identity development
- Cass (1979) and D'Augelli (1991) on gay, lesbian, bisexual, and transgender identity development

Outcomes for psychosocial identity are divided into two groups: the self and the relational. Student growth in these areas within college is affected by multiple and often intersecting factors: curricular influences like experiences in the classroom, socialization in the major field, diversity courses such as women's studies and ethnic studies, and service-learning courses like internships. Influences outside class include interaction with faculty and peers, diversity experiences, racial/cultural awareness workshops, perceptions of campus climate, and participation in student activities, clubs, sports, and Greek letter organizations, among others.

Other Noncognitive Student Outcomes. Various members of society are calling for college graduates to have many personal and interpersonal attributes rather than just a mastery of knowledge in their major fields. Some of these outcomes include ethical behaviors and decisions, character development, spirituality, civic responsibility, teamwork and collaboration, interpersonal communication, public speaking and presentation skills, and the ability to work in diverse groups or settings.

These outcomes are largely products of student affairs and campus activities, but they are beginning to creep into classroom learning outcomes statements as well. Student affairs professionals have been working to provide growth on these outcomes for many years and know how to do this, but assessment of these abilities is imperative and lagging. In addition, partnerships between faculty and student affairs professionals can help faculty learn how to create classroom environments that foster development in these areas so that students' experiences in and out of the classroom truly are complementary. Institutional researchers should not waste their efforts in reinventing the wheel and should make every attempt to use the experiences gained by the student affairs professionals.

Chickering's Seven Vector Theory of Identity Development. Chickering's theory of identity development is perhaps the best known and most widely cited. Chickering (1969) and later Chickering and Reisser (1993) proposed that students move through seven vectors psychosocially:

- *Achieving competence:* Intellectual, physical, and interpersonal growth
- *Managing emotions:* Ability to recognize and accept emotions
- *Moving through autonomy toward interdependence:* Freedom from the constant approval of others toward emotional independence
- *Developing mature interpersonal relationships:* Increased acceptance of others and a respect and appreciation for their differences
- *Establishing identity:* Comprehension of previous vectors, as well as a deeper understanding of one's gender, ethnic background, and sexual orientation
- *Developing purpose:* Establishing clear goals and strategically following through with them even when challenges arise

- *Developing integrity:* Three sequential stages of humanizing values (struggle of self/others to balance of self/others), personalizing values (acceptance of core beliefs and acknowledgment of the beliefs of others), and developing congruence (actions correlate with beliefs and is demonstrated through civic duties).

Chickering (1969) purposely did not call each phase a stage, because he believed people could experience each vector simultaneously. He labeled them vectors "because each seems to have direction and magnitude—even though the direction may be expressed more appropriately by a spiral or by steps than by a straight line" (p. 8). His initial theory was based on research that he conducted with college men at the end of their sophomore and senior years. He gathered information from achievement tests, personality, assessments, student journals, and interviews.

Personal Growth Assessment Instruments

This section provides a summary of assessment tools that campuses may find useful in measuring students' personal development. In each case, we describe the instrument and its uses. However, these instruments generally have many advantages and disadvantages in common.

Common Advantages
- Collecting student self-reported college experiences and outcomes are less costly than attempting to measure student learning directly.
- Most tools are offered in both on-line and paper-based formats with scoring services.
- They have established reliability.
- They provide normative data for comparison with other institutions.
- Most request student identification numbers for merger with institutional data for follow-up studies.
- They are easily completed within a normal class session.
- They contain space for locally designed additional questions.
- The instruments are marketed by their publishers as providing useful results for accreditation and self-study reports, campus planning, and policy analysis.

Common Disadvantages
- They consist of self-reported, indirect measures of student outcomes. Although they are generally accurate for measuring the aggregated outcomes for groups of students, self-reported information is less reliable for individuals, some of whom may choose to give what they think are preferred rather than truthful answers (see Chapter Ten).
- They lack institution-specific customization, although this is somewhat ameliorated by the additional questions that may be added locally.

NEW DIRECTIONS FOR INSTITUTIONAL RESEARCH • DOI: 10.1002/ir

- Students have the option of omitting their identification information, although this limits the instrument's usefulness since responses cannot be definitely tied to local information for all students.

ACT Survey Services. ACT provides a number of two-year and four-year college surveys, but in our view, the most useful of these ACT surveys for assessing student cognitive and noncognitive outcomes is the College Outcomes Survey (COS). The ACT Student Opinion Survey (SOS) is useful for assessing student satisfaction. The COS and the SOS are described below.

ACT also publishes a variety of surveys that are useful for evaluating student needs, student services, student support programs, and facilities. These include the Adult Learner Needs Assessment Survey, College Students Needs Assessment Survey, Entering Student Survey, Student Opinion Survey (four-year and two-year versions), Survey of Current Activities and Plans, Survey of Academic Advising, Financial Aid Student Services Survey, Survey of Post-secondary Education Plans, and Withdrawing/Non-returning Student Survey (long and short forms). The various entering student and needs assessment surveys are most appropriate for measuring student inputs and needs rather than outcomes. In addition, ACT publishes at least three alumni surveys that include a mix of self-reported outcomes and evaluations of the undergraduate experience, and these are discussed in the next chapter.

College Outcomes Survey. The COS (http://www.act.org/ess/pdf/College Outcomes.pdf) collects an array of student information for assessing student growth, as well as student academic and social adjustment. The instrument contains over eighty items for students to assess the importance of, progress toward, and college contribution to their growth and development. We judged over forty of these items to reflect noncognitive growth and likely to be learned outside, as well as inside, the classroom. In addition, forty-eight items assess student satisfaction with selected aspects of the institution's programs, services, and campus climate. This four-page instrument is valuable for researchers because it includes an extensive set of questions about student backgrounds, sources of support, college impressions and plans, and responsibilities on- and off-campus.

Student Opinion Survey (Two-Year and Four-Year versions). The SOS (http://www.act.org/ess/pdf/SurveyofStudentOpinions.pdf) is a robust satisfaction survey that assesses students' perceptions about a wide range of programs, services, and environmental factors at the college they are attending. This is a useful survey if student satisfaction is considered to be an important outcome. Also included is an extensive set of questions about student backgrounds, sources of support, and college impressions. Only five items ask students to assess their growth.

College Student Experiences Questionnaire and Community College Student Experiences Questionnaire. These instruments measure campus climate and student effort and outcomes. Originally developed by

Robert Pace and based on his theories of engagement and involvement, the instruments include sections on background information, the college environment including activities and interactions, measures of student effort including classroom experiences and reading and writing, and estimation of students' gains on several dimensions.

College Student Experiences Questionnaire. The College Student Experiences Questionnaire (CSEQ; http://cseq.iub.edu/cseq_generalinfo.cfm) measures three general aspects of a student's experience: (1) college activities (student quality of effort toward campus resources and opportunities for learning and development), (2) college environment (student opinions about the priorities and emphases of the campus environment), and (3) estimate of gains (student self-reported progress toward a diverse range of educational outcomes). Administered since 1979, the instrument has a long track record with established validity and reliability. The research literature contains hundreds of studies using the CSEQ. The survey results can be used for measuring learning outcomes, student involvement in a variety of campus initiatives, program effectiveness, and impact of campus environment.

Community College Student Experiences Questionnaire. Like the CSEQ, the Community College Student Experiences Questionnaire (CCSEQ; http://coe.memphis.edu/CSHE/CCSEQ.htm) is designed to measure the quality of effort that students invest in their college experiences. The instrument focuses on four distinct elements:

- Who are the community college students, and why are they attending college?
- Which facilities and opportunities at the community college do students use productively and extensively?
- What are the students' impressions of the community college?
- What progress have students made toward their stated goals?

The survey results can be used for evaluating general education, transfer, and vocational programs alike.

The Cooperative Institutional Research Program. The Cooperative Institutional Research Program (CIRP) was developed by the Higher Education Research Institute at the University of California at Los Angeles. We review here three CIRP surveys: The Freshman Survey, Your First College Year, and College Student Survey.

The Freshman Survey. The Freshman Survey (TFS; http://www.gseis.ucla.edu/heri/cirpoverview.php) has been administered since 1966 and is designed to provide comprehensive information on incoming first-year students, including their readiness for college, factors in their college choice, values and beliefs, and college expectations. The survey is useful for measuring student characteristics at entry but not for measuring college outcomes. However, it can provide baseline data and be used in conjunction with the following two CIRP surveys for a longitudinal assessment.

Your First College Year. Your First College Year (YFCY; http://www.gseis.ucla.edu/heri/yfcyOverview.php) survey, designed as a follow-up survey to the TFS, assesses academic and personal development of students over the first year of college. About one-third of the items on the instrument are posttest questions from the TFS, thus allowing institutions to examine how aspects of student behavior, beliefs, and identity change during the first year of college. The strength of YFCY is the self-reported assessment of learning outcomes, attitudes, and behaviors across numerous cognitive and affective measures.

College Student Survey. College Student Survey (CSS; http://www.gseis.ucla.edu/heri/cssoverview.php) is typically administered to senior students or used as an exit survey. It covers a broad range of outcomes, including academic achievement and engagement; satisfaction with the college experience; student involvement; cognitive and affective development; student values, attitudes, and goals; degree aspirations and career plans; and Internet and other technology use. CSS can be used to study the impact of service learning, leadership development, and student-faculty interactions, as well as to assess a wide variety of student assessment practices. In addition, the latest version of the survey offers feedback on students' postcollege plans immediately following graduation.

College Adjustment Scales. College Adjustment Scales (CAS; http://www3.parinc.com/products/product.aspx?Productid=CAS_COLLEGE) is designed to assess how well students are adjusting to the demands of college and university life. The survey is primarily intended for use in college counseling and guidance centers. Subscales include depression, anxiety, suicidal ideation, effects of substance abuse, self-esteem problems, interpersonal problems, family problems, academic problems, and career choice problems. Other instruments available on the Web site include the Coping Responses Inventory and the Minnesota Multiphasic Personality Inventory. CAS is targeted at college students in their teens and early twenties, so it may not be suitable for older college students.

Educational Planning Survey. Penn State's Educational Planning Survey (EPS; http://www.psu.edu/dus/eps/) is designed to enhance and expedite the initial advisement meeting and improve academic advising by collecting information about the entering student's background, high school academic and out-of-class experiences, expectations about college, educational and occupational plans, and reasons for attending college. The survey helps students reflect on previous educational experiences, areas of strength and weakness, educational goals, and potential major and program of studies. There are no national norms.

Learning and Study Strategies Inventory. The Learning and Study Strategies Inventory (LASSI; http://www.hhpublishing.com/_assessments/LASSI/index.html) is designed to measure students' strengths and weaknesses in ten areas causally related to academic success: attitude, motivation, time management, anxiety, concentration, information processing, selecting main ideas, study aids, self-testing, and testing strategies. It provides standardized scores that can be both diagnostic and prescriptive in each of the ten areas. It can be used as a counseling tool aimed at student development or as an evaluation tool to assess the degree of success of intervention programs or courses. The test is self-scoring for immediate feedback and available in English and Spanish.

National Survey of Student Engagement and Community College Survey of Student Engagement. The National Survey of Student Engagement and Community College Survey of Student Engagement are research-based instruments designed to collect information about student participation in, and outcomes of, programs and activities that institutions provide for their learning and personal development. Developed by a national group of higher education scholars led by George Kuh, they contain items that attempt to operationalize the Chickering and Gamson seven good practices in undergraduate education. Survey sections include college activities, college environment, estimate of gains, opinions about the institution, and background information.

National Survey of Student Engagement. The National Survey of Student Engagement (NSSE; http://nsse.iub.edu/html/about.cfm)is administered to freshmen and seniors during the spring semester. Results are organized into five national benchmarks of effective educational practice: level of academic challenge, active and collaborative learning, student-faculty interaction, enriching educational experiences, and supportive campus environment. A strength of the survey is its strong research base with established validity and reliability, designed to reflect undergraduate curricular and cocurricular experiences via student reports. Workshops are available to help institutions better use NSSE results to enhance good practices in undergraduate education. In addition to developing best practices internally, NSSE data can also be used to communicate information to external stakeholders.

Community College Survey of Student Engagement. The community college counterpart of NSSE, Community College Survey of Student Engagement (CCSSE; http://www.ccsse.org/) is designed to assess student engagement and outcomes in community colleges. Like NSSE, it asks students about their involvement in academic and out-of-class activities; their interaction with faculty, staff, and peers; estimates of gains; and the subject matter in their courses.

Perceptions, Expectations, Emotions, and Knowledge About College. Perceptions, Expectations, Emotions, and Knowledge About College

(PEEK; http://www.hhpublishing.com/_assessments/PEEK/index.html) is designed to assess students' reactions to personal, social, and academic changes that may occur in a college setting. It evolved from work on the Cognitive Learning Strategies Project at the University of Texas at Austin. Although there are no national norms, institutions can track their own improvement by repeated administrations over time. The survey contains items in three categories:

- *Academic experiences,* which cover expectations of faculty, kind of learning and study necessary in college, and academic success or difficulties
- *Personal experiences,* which cover such things as clarity of goals for education, expectations for challenge in college, and expectations of success or failure in college
- *Social experiences,* which include expectations of college social relations, diversity of student body, and continuing relations with family and friends

Gathering the type of information in the PEEK survey may help to inform admissions in terms of understanding the types of students who are not a good fit.

Conclusion

In this chapter, we have described some of the most widely used surveys for assessing noncognitive outcomes among large populations of undergraduates. As discussed further in Chapter Ten, a growing body of research over the past twenty years supports the adequacy of self-reported measures as proxies for objective measures of the same traits or skills. Moreover, there now are hundreds of studies indicating that student engagement, involvement, and effort are strongly associated with positive outcomes like student learning (Kuh, Pace, and Vesper, 1997; Kuh, 2001; Pascarella, Cruce, Umbach, Wolniak, Kuh, Carini, et al., 2006; Pascarella and Terenzini, 2005; Porter, 2006; Volkwein, 2007). Since these conditions that foster student learning are easier to measure than student learning itself, these instruments have been developed to collect data on student involvement, commitment, engagement, effort, and good educational practices as outcomes that are easily measured. All of these instruments are useful for the collection of self-reported student experiences, involvement, effort, and gains.

References

Astin, A. W., Panos, R. J., and Creager, J. A. *National Norms for Entering College Freshmen—Fall 1966.* Washington, DC: American Council on Education, 1967.

Banta, T. W., Lund, J. P., Black, K. E., and Oblander, F. W. (eds.). *Assessment in Practice: Putting Principles to Work on College Campuses.* San Francisco: Jossey-Bass, 1996.

Cass, V. C. "Homosexual Identity Formation: A Theoretical Model." *Journal of Homosexuality,* 1979, 4, 219–235.

Chickering, A. *Education and Identity*. San Francisco: Jossey-Bass, 1969.

Chickering, A., and Reisser, L. *Education and Identity*. (2nd ed.) San Francisco: Jossey-Bass, 1993.

Cross, W. E., Jr. "The Psychology of Nigrescence: Revising the Cross Model." In J. G. Ponterott, J. M. Casas, L. A. Suzuki, and C. M. Alexander (eds.), *Handbook of Multicultural Counseling*. Thousand Oaks, CA: Sage, 1995.

D'Augelli, A. R. "Gay Men in College: Identity Processes and Adaptations." *Journal of College Student Development*, 1991, *32*, 140–146.

Helms, J. E. "An Update of Helms' White and People of Color Racial Identity Models." In J. G. Ponterott, J. M. Casas, L. A. Suzuki, and C. M. Alexander (eds.), *Handbook of Multicultural Counseling*. Thousand Oaks, CA: Sage, 1995.

Josselson, R. *Finding Herself: Pathways to Identity Development in Women*. San Francisco: Jossey-Bass, 1987.

Kuh, G. D. "Assessing What Really Matters to Student Learning: Inside the National Survey of Student Engagement." *Change*, 2001, *33*(3), 10–17, 66.

Kuh, G. D., Pace, C. R., and Vesper, N. "The Development of Process Indicators to Estimate Student Gains Associated with Good Practices in Undergraduate Education." *Research in Higher Education*, 1997, *38*(4), 435–454.

Pascarella, E. T., Cruce, T., Umbach, P. D., Wolniak, G. C., Kuh, G. D., Carini, R. M., et al. "Institutional Selectivity and Good Practices in Undergraduate Education: How Strong Is the Link?" *Journal of Higher Education*, 2006, *77*(2), 251–285.

Pascarella, E. T., and Terenzini, P. T. *How College Affects Students: A Third Decade of Research*. San Francisco: Jossey-Bass, 2005.

Phinney, J. S. "Ethnic Identity in Adolescents and Adults: Review of the Research." *Psychological Bulletin*, 1990, *108*, 499–514.

Porter, S. R. "Institutional Structures and Student Engagement." *Research in Higher Education*, 2006, *47*(5), 521–558.

Volkwein, J. F. "Assessing Institutional Effectiveness and Connecting the Pieces of a Fragmented University." In J. C. Burke (ed.), *Fixing the Fragmented University*. San Francisco: Jossey-Bass/Anker, 2007.

Yanikoski, R. "Leadership Perspectives on the Role of Character Development in Higher Education." In J. Dalton, T. Russell, and S. Kline (eds.), *Assessing Character Outcomes in College*. New Directions for Institutional Research, no. 122. San Francisco: Jossey-Bass, 2004.

Recommended Reading

Astin, A. W. *What Matters in College? Four Critical Years Revisited*. San Francisco: Jossey-Bass, 1993.

Borden, V., and Zak Owens, J. *Measuring Quality: Choosing Among Surveys and Other College and University Quality Assessments*. Washington, DC: Association for Institutional Research and American Council on Education, 2001. Retrieved March 4, 2010, from http://www.airweb.org/images/measurequality.pdf.

Erikson, E. H. *Identity: Youth and Crisis*. New York: Norton, 1994.

Kuh, G. D. "Imagine Asking the Client: Using Student and Alumni Surveys for Accountability in Higher Education." In J. Burke (ed.), *Achieving Accountability in Higher Education: Balancing Public, Academic, and Market Demands*. San Francisco: Jossey-Bass, 2005.

Reason, R., and Lutovsky, B. "Psychosocial Development and Non-Cognitive Student Outcomes." PowerPoint presentation, *Studying Students and Student Affairs Programs*, Pennsylvania State University, 2006.

Shenkle, C. W., Snyder, R. S., and Bauer, K. W. "Measures of Campus Climate." In K. Bauer (ed.), *Campus Climate: Understanding the Critical Components of Today's Col-*

leges and Universities. New Directions for Institutional Research, no. 98. San Francisco: Jossey-Bass, 1998.

Strange, C. "Measuring Up: Defining and Assessing Outcomes of Character in College." In J. Dalton, T. Russell, and S. Kline (eds.), *Assessing Character Outcomes in College.* New Directions for Institutional Research, no. 122. San Francisco: Jossey-Bass, 2004.

Strauss, L. C., and Volkwein, J. F. "Predictors of Student Commitment at Two-Year and Four-Year Institutions." *Journal of Higher Education,* 2004, 75(2), 203–227.

Schuh, J. H., and Upcraft, M. L. *Assessment Practice in Student Affairs: An Applications Manual.* San Francisco: Jossey-Bass, 2001.

Upcraft, M. L., and Schuh, J. H. *Assessment in Student Affairs: A Guide for Practitioners.* San Francisco: Jossey-Bass, 1996.

YING (JESSIE) LIU is a Ph.D. candidate in the Higher Education Program, the Pennsylvania State University.

ALEXANDER C. YIN is a senior project associate of the Center for the Study of Higher Education at The Pennsylvania State University.

9

Evaluative statements from alumni have legitimacy with both internal and external stakeholders. Thus, alumni studies can provide valuable evidence of institutional effectiveness and lend themselves to both locally designed and commercial survey instruments for data collection.

Assessing Alumni Outcomes

J. Fredericks Volkwein

Colleges and universities customarily survey their graduates in order to collect subsequent education and career information and to cultivate charitable giving and volunteering. As early as the 1930s, leading colleges surveyed alumni to track their professional degree attainment and collect information on workforce issues and employment (Pace, 1979). During the remainder of the twentieth century, the purposes of alumni research multiplied and proliferated across the full range of institution types (Pettit and Litten, 1999).

In recent decades, institutions of higher education increasingly view their alumni as valuable sources of both information and financial support. Alumni offer important perspectives for evaluating academic programs and student services and are often used in student recruitment and mentoring. Alumni giving now occupies a prominent position in the modern strategic plan. In the past twenty years, more and more campuses have used alumni surveys to assess the impact of the collegiate experience on student cognitive and noncognitive development (Cabrera, Weerts, and Zulick, 2005). The standards of most regional and specialized accreditors now call for outcomes evidence and using assessment feedback for educational and administrative improvement (Volkwein, 2007). Moreover, colleges and universities are beginning to incorporate feedback from alumni in performance and accountability systems (Borden, 2005; Ewell, 2005). These trends also appear to be developing in some European countries (Weerts and Vidal, 2005).

New Directions for Institutional Research, Assessment Supplement 2009, Spring 2010   © Wiley Periodicals, Inc.
Published online in Wiley InterScience (www.interscience.wiley.com) • DOI: 10.1002/ir.335

Value of Alumni Studies

When visiting campuses to discuss assessment, I always identify alumni studies as the most cost-effective way to begin a program of outcomes assessment. Compared to many other forms of data collection, an alumni study, using a survey instrument, can be a relatively inexpensive way to gather an array of outcomes information that is useful at institutional and departmental levels alike.

Alumni provide a Janusian perspective both internal and external to the organization (Volkwein, 1989, 1999). Graduating seniors and alumni can provide the same feedback, but the faculty is likely to discount the views of seniors as being uninformed, whereas they attribute great authority to the same opinions by alumni.

Evaluative statements from alumni and employers have legitimacy with both internal and external stakeholders. Internally, alumni studies can assess important outcomes and provide information for enhancing academic curricula, support programs, and administrative policy. Externally, alumni studies can support accreditation, accountability, recruitment, and fundraising. Such studies provide opportunities for faculty and administrative collaboration because faculty and staff interests in alumni outcomes coincide. Alumni surveys typically have space for both institutional and department questions, so multiple purposes can be served from one data collection. Alumni studies are at their best when they are characterized by centralized data collection and decentralized uses of the data.

Typical Alumni Outcomes

The list below contains a summary of the information that is typically collected by alumni surveys, assembled from the following scholars: Borden (2005), Cabrera et al. (2005), Delaney (2004), Moden and Williford (1988), Murray (1994), Pace (1979), Pettit and Litten (1999), Schneider and Niederjohn (1995), Volkwein (1989), Volkwein and Bian (1990, 1999), Volkwein and Parmley (1999), and Weerts and Vidal (2005). Ideally, the alumni researcher begins with entry-level demographic, family, educational, and precollege characteristics, so these do not need to be collected each time alumni are contacted. The following are common contents in the typical alumni survey:

Collegiate Experiences
- Campus participation in extramural activities and clubs, athletics and recreation, student media, fraternities and sororities, service organizations, and residential life
- Student government participation and leadership
- Civic and community engagement off-campus
- Multicultural activities and tolerance for diversity
- Financial aid received and accumulated loan debt

NEW DIRECTIONS FOR INSTITUTIONAL RESEARCH • DOI: 10.1002/ir

- Quality of instruction received
- Enhanced abilities and knowledge
- Satisfaction with various academic and collegiate experiences
- Perceived college impact on personal development
- Perceived college impact on professional development
- Preparation for graduate school
- Preparation for career and employment
- General satisfaction with the institution
- Overall evaluation of the undergraduate experience
- Willingness to enroll again in the same institution

Postgraduation Outcomes
- Additional education and degrees earned
- Occupation and career attainment
- Occupation and career satisfaction
- Socioeconomic status
- Personal and household income
- Professional and community leadership and service
- Awards and recognition

Alumni Participation and Support
- Alumni organization membership
- Participation in alumni events, activities, mentoring, and recruitment
- Alumni association leadership
- Frequency and amount of alumni giving

The diversity of this list reflects the evolution of alumni studies from simple descriptions of the alumni population to analytical outcomes studies. The outcomes approach to assessment assumes that institutional quality and effectiveness are at least partly based on what alumni accomplish after leaving the institution, controlling for their characteristics on entry. Moreover, researchers now recognize that the potential outcomes of the collegiate experience range from the academic to the personal, from acquired knowledge to ethical behavior, from social skills to career satisfaction, from earned degrees to earned income. Thus, alumni studies seek to collect information on the full range of student collegiate and postcollegiate experiences.

Under ideal conditions, the results of alumni studies equip faculty and administrators with information for making constructive alterations to programs and curricula, as well as for demonstrating institutional effectiveness. However, several research challenges must be addressed.

Challenging Problems with Alumni Studies

Challenge 1: Which Alumni Do You Survey? Alumni surveys serve different purposes, and each purpose requires different populations and different survey content. Assessment for curricular and program improvement needs feedback from recent graduates. Assessing the student experience and the current academic program should be undertaken while memories of the experience are fresh. Surveys of recent graduates also have the advantage of tracking the graduates as they enter their first jobs and are developing sympathetic habits of mind toward their alma mater.

Assessing educational attainment, however, requires at least a ten-year period for undergraduate alumni to complete advanced degrees in graduate and professional school. Although many alumni enter their first job within a year of graduation, a sizable number delay their entry into the job market while they pursue master's or doctoral degrees, or even military service. And it is not uncommon for some doctoral students in humanities, education, and social sciences to finish their programs after more than ten years.

Assessment for purposes of measuring career outcomes requires an even longer time frame than measuring educational outcomes. It may take thirty or forty years to accumulate a significant record of career accomplishment, honors, awards, civic engagement, and professional or even political leadership. But the institution is likely to have changed a great deal after that many years, so the assessment of older alumni may provide little relevant information for current faculty, curricula, student life, administrative services, and campus climate. One exception may be the general education program. Although department curricula and faculty may change with each generation, older alumni may have wisdom to share about the content of the general education curriculum based on their life experiences.

Thus, the purpose of the alumni study needs clarity before the population is targeted and the survey designed. If the research has a formative purpose, aimed at evaluating and improving curricula, services, and facilities, then a younger population should be targeted. But if the alumni study has a more summative purpose, aimed at gathering evidence of outcomes, then an older population is required. One should not expect young alumni in the aggregate to exhibit community leadership and professional honors, nor should older alumni be expected to evaluate current student services and facilities in an informed way.

Challenge 2: What Alumni Sample Size? You do not need a large, expensive sample to adequately represent the views of the alumni population, so you can carry out most alumni surveys inexpensively with small but representative samples. However, the main value of alumni studies is bringing data to the department level, where the improvement potential is greatest. Ideally the alumni sample needs to yield enough responses to break out the data by academic department, at least for the largest departments. Thus, the need for disaggregating the data may drive up the sample size and the cost.

However, the majority of departments have a small number of graduates in any given year, especially in fine arts, languages, literature, and area studies, but also in some math, science, and professional school departments. Thus, you may need to invest in a survey that aggregates large numbers of alumni across many graduation years in order to have enough cases to provide anything useful to most departments. Moreover, if you present data only at the campus level, rather than disaggregating them to the department level, faculty can exercise denial, as in, "That's not true for my department." Most researchers recommend twenty-five responses per department as a healthy target; fewer than ten not only threatens anonymity but also prevents most multivariate procedures from including academic department as a variable in the analysis.

Challenge 3: Frequency of Data Collection? Although the institution may want to collect contact and placement information from recent graduates almost every year, I suggest conducting alumni outcomes studies no more than once every four or five years. Launching a multipurpose survey every year and attempting to circulate results produces redundant overload, especially for academic departments and administrative services. Alumni attitudes in the aggregate, from one graduating cohort to the next, change very slowly, if at all, over a long period of time—unless there is an institutional scandal or catastrophe. Moreover, academic organizations are notorious for having slow response cycles, so the process of alumni research design, data collection, statistical analyses, campus communication, administrative digestion of results, and curricular and programmatic actions can take several years to play out. Undertaking another survey while all this is going on gains little.

Longitudinal analyses and trends over time provide some of the most valuable outcomes evidence. But if you survey the same people too frequently, they will stop responding. To avoid survey saturation, I recommend surveying the same alumni no more than once a decade and asking respondents each time how much their opinion has changed since they graduated. This provides *ex post facto* longitudinal data.

Challenge 4: What Response Scales Should You Use? Like other assessment efforts, the most useful alumni research moves beyond simple descriptions of the population and attempts to examine relationships and causal connections using multivariate analysis. Reporting descriptive statistics requires only high, medium, and low kinds of responses, but to facilitate multivariate analyses and examine relationships, you need to spread out the data and maximize variation. When collecting evaluative judgments, such as levels of satisfaction, involvement, importance, frequency, and adequacy, I strongly recommend using (at a minimum) a five-point Likert-type scale. Some researchers use seven, nine, and even ten response categories to support scale building and multivariate analysis.

The proper response scale is particularly important when asking about personal and household income. Some researchers try to separate the financial and educational outcomes data collections, and perhaps use proxies for income (such as postal codes and job titles). But most college graduates know that the institution is interested in their support and know that the survey is being used for multiple purposes. Obviously a survey needs to give respondents the option of not completing items that they do not wish to, and most people are reluctant to divulge specific personal and household income. However, my own experience is that 98 percent of alumni are willing to indicate their incomes in ten or twelve large categories (for example, twenty-thousand-dollar increments in the lower ranges and fifty-thousand-dollar increments in the higher ranges), and this is usually adequate variation to use in a multivariate outcomes analysis.

Challenge #5: Survey Length and Content

Length. What is the recommended survey length? Although there's no silver bullet (and every population is a little different), you will usually get the best response by aiming for the middle of each population. You first have to think through your survey goals, but assuming that you want at least *some* demographics, and *some* campus experiences, and *some* alumni outcomes, aim for a maximum of one page of questions on each. A total survey of two pages probably provides too little information, three pages is ideal, the back and front of two pages (4 sides) is okay, five pages starts to dampen responses. Almost everyone now recommends giving respondents the choice of on-line or hard copy response modes as a way to increase responses.

Content. Every survey researcher knows that constructing a good instrument is demanding, and starting with a blank page is rarely the best alternative for a campus. Purchasing a commercial survey or building your own collaboratively with other institutions is often cost-effective. Several institutional consortia and university systems have constructed joint surveys and shared their findings. But if you are an alumni researcher building your own survey, how much can be borrowed from other surveys and how should you give proper credit?

Earlier in my career, I collected all the published collegiate surveys and was surprised to see a high degree of similarity among those copyrighted by ACT, HERI/CIRP, HEDS, CUES, NCHEMS, CSEQ, and now NSSE. Although the response scales vary from one to another, the basic thrust of many of these surveys is highly similar with only minor changes in wording. I believe this happened in part because the same small group of researchers (Stern, Pace, Astin, Pascarella, Terenzini) developed the early concepts and items, and in part because no one really wants to litigate intellectual property rights with professional colleagues. What we have now is a polite understanding that locally developed campus surveys are generally not copyrighted and campuses can borrow a few items or scales from each other without being challenged. Obviously, it is improper to copy whole sections word-for-word (at least not without first obtaining permission to do so and acknowledging the authoring institution somewhere). Even ACT generally grants permission to use selected items or even entire scales with proper acknowledgment. Obviously, the problem is not with demographic items—there are a limited number of ways to gather background data like age, race, sex, family characteristics, and schooling. But using half or more of any scale purporting to measure such attributes as learning outcomes, satisfaction, attitudes, or values without acknowledgment will attract some negative attention.

Challenge #6: Alumni GIGO. The impacts of colleges and universities on their students have received a good deal of attention in the research literature (see Pascarella and Terenzini, 2005). Although college experiences and degree completion exert significant influences, student and family characteristics on entry also explain many differences in subsequent outcomes. Since "good-in/good-out" is a reality, student and alumni outcomes studies need to make statistical adjustments for entering student and family characteristics, especially when the research examines financial and occupational outcomes, but also when other variables like test scores are treated as outcomes of the undergraduate experience. Those with higher admissions test scores as freshmen are more likely to have higher Graduate Record Exam and professional school admissions test scores as seniors, at least in the aggregate. Students from highly educated and affluent families are more likely to become highly educated and affluent alumni (Astin, 1977, 1993; Blau and Duncan, 1967; Bowen, 1977; Feldman and Newcomb, 1969; Pace, 1979; Sewell and Hauser, 1975).

Personal and family characteristics, educational experiences, degree attainment, hard work, motivation, judgment, and luck all combine to produce occupational achievement and socioeconomic status. In order to demonstrate the institution's impact on its alumni, the researcher should include as many of these variables as possible in a multivariate analysis that statistically isolates the influence of each variable on the particular outcome. Using a causal model constitutes one of the best ways to conceptualize and organize such an outcomes research project.

Begin the Alumni Study with a Model

In Chapters Two through Four, we make the case for using an outcomes model for guiding research design, data collection, and analysis. A variety of models are relevant to the undergraduate outcomes examined in this volume (basic skills, general education, attainment in the major, personal growth). The Terenzini-Reason Comprehensive Model and the Albany Outcomes Model are among those that provide good roadmaps for assessment. The Albany model identifies not only an array of collegiate outcomes, but a group of alumni outcomes as well. As shown in Figure 4.2, the model suggests that alumni outcomes such as graduate degrees earned, occupational status and income, career satisfaction, job performance, leadership, awards, and alumni giving are each influenced by a collection of personal and family traits, precollege achievement and motivation, academic and social college experiences, and educational and personal outcomes. These different traits and experiences collectively combine to produce an array of variable outcomes. During the 1980s and 1990s, the Office of Institutional Research at the State University of New York at Albany developed measures for each of the components in the model. This empirical research served as important evidence of institutional effectiveness in the Albany self-study documents for Middle States Accreditation in 1990 and 2000.

Sometimes researchers find it useful to develop a separate conceptual model for each outcome. For example, Volkwein (1989) focused on one component of the Albany Outcomes Model and developed a separate model of alumni giving, shown in Figure 9.1. (Also see Volkwein and Parmley, 1999).

As state appropriations and financial support from private foundations and industry become less dependable, higher education institutions seek alumni contributions as alternative sources of funding. Drawing on both the fundraising and the outcomes assessment literature, the Volkwein model treats alumni giving behavior as a desirable outcome. The amounts and frequency of alumni giving are functions of both the capacity to give and the motivation to do so. However, the attitudes and values that produce motivation, and the economic attainment and achievements that produce capacity, are themselves the products of the backgrounds and collegiate experiences of alumni. The model incorporates concepts from all these various branches of the literature in an attempt to explain alumni generosity toward the institution. Alumni researchers can use this model to show campus managers and faculty the clear connections between their actions and subsequent support for the institution.

By applying the model to its alumni population, an institution is likely to discover that some traits and experiences exert greater influences on alumni giving behavior than others. Precollege background characteristics are more distant from the actual alumni behavior than the college and post-college variables, but early indicators of student talent and family wealth are likely to be influential. Private institutions certainly place a high value on them in their student recruitment. The student outcomes literature suggests that college experiences and outcomes on the campus, the curricular and the extracurricular alike, shape student and alumni attitudes and achievements. The financial development and fundraising literature focuses on the importance of alumni involvement, satisfaction, volunteer service, and income. Thinking about all the little things that add up to creating motivation and capacity encourages faculty, administrators, and fundraisers alike to shape their daily campus actions in ways that support the long-term financial health of the institution.

Another relevant model treats socioeconomic achievement as a collegiate outcome. Smart and Pascarella (1986) developed a path model (Figure 9.2) to examine the impact of various precollege characteristics, institutional characteristics, and campus experiences on the socioeconomic achievements of a 1980 population that entered college in 1971. Finding

Figure 9.1. Volkwein Model of Alumni Giving

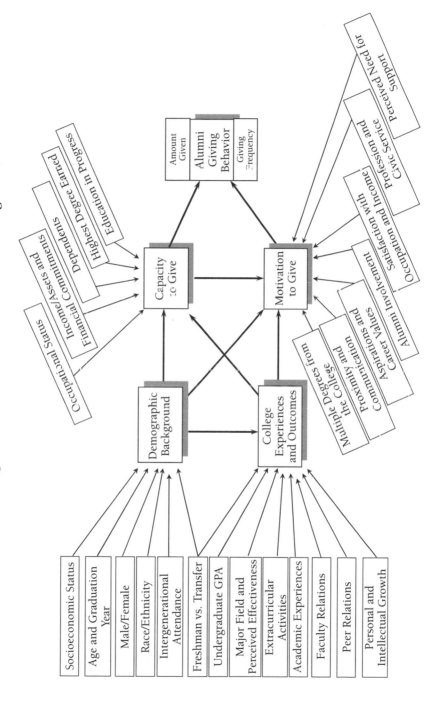

modest support for their model, they found that a scale measuring student academic integration in college proved to be the strongest and most consistent predictor of socioeconomic attainment across male and female, white and minority populations. Although family origins exerted significant influences, these generally were outweighed by collegiate experiences and choices, especially academic ones. Their model is multi-institutional rather than single, so it may have important implications for a variety of institution types.

Sources of Information for Alumni Researchers

Despite the growing importance of alumni outcomes research, only a small number of national and state resources have been developed to assist researchers, and there has been little national benchmarking by institution type. Two attempts to develop a national instrument and database have been discontinued—one by the National Center for Higher Education Management systems and the other by the National Center for Postsecondary Improvement. National public sources of information include the following:

- The U.S. Bureau of Labor Statistics maintains comparative data and statistical reports on occupations and employment from national surveys. http://www.bls.gov/oes/home.htm.
- The National Center for Education Statistics conducts longitudinal studies containing information on educational and occupational attainment of high school and college graduates. http://nces.ed.gov/surveys/Survey Groups.asp?Group=2.

Figure 9.2. Smart and Pascarella Causal Model of Socioeconomic Achievement

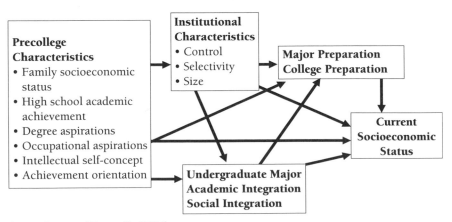

Source: Smart and Pascarella (1986).

- The National Association for Colleges and Employers surveys job and salary outcomes of college graduates that can be used for benchmarking. http://www.naceweb.org/Research.aspx.

Several higher education organizations and consortia have developed surveys that member institutions can administer to their alumni and share comparative data. The most prominent of these collaborations are:

- The Council for Advancement and Support of Education provides member institutions in fifty-nine countries with data, products, and services in alumni relations, communications, development, marketing, and advancement. For example, its collaboration with the Association for Institutional Research resulted in a compendium of articles on campus-based alumni research (Shoemaker, 1999). http://www.case.org/About_CASE.html.
- The Higher Education Data Sharing (HEDS) consortium has 160 relatively selective private colleges and universities as members. HEDS shares data and conducts comparative research on behalf of its members, and the HEDS alumni survey is considered to be well designed and multipurpose. http://www.e-heds.org.
- The Appalachian College Association (ACA) is a consortium of thirty-three private colleges and universities situated in eastern Kentucky, western North Carolina, eastern Tennessee, southwestern Virginia, and West Virginia. Using Patrick Terenzini and Ernie Pascarella as consultants, the ACA developed and administered an alumni survey copyrighted by The American College Testing organization. http://www.acaweb.org/content.aspx?sid=1&pid=73.
- The American Association for Universities Data Exchange comprises AAU institutions that participate in the exchange of data and information to support decision making at their institutions. http://aaude.org.

Some state university systems, such as those in Illinois, New York, and North Carolina, have conducted systemwide surveys. The best of these is the survey developed by ACT for the State University of New York System.

As of December 2009, the best assemblage of multipurpose alumni comparative data is embedded in the norms maintained by the publisher of the leading commercial instruments: the American College Testing Program (ACT; http://www.act.org/ess/postsec.html). ACT offers a choice of two alumni survey instruments for four-year institutions of higher education (http://www.act.org/ess/fouryear.html) and two for two-year institutions (http://www.act.org/ess/twoyear.html). It developed and holds copyrights to the instruments now used by the State University of New York and the consortium of Appalachian Region Colleges, among others. These ACT surveys generally contain a group of twelve to twenty demographic and background items, including reasons for attendance and sources of funding; twenty to thirty self-reported educational outcomes, ranging from problem solving and critical thinking to teamwork and communications skills; twenty to forty items reflecting levels of satisfaction with educational and campus experiences, services, and facilities; ten to twenty items describing levels of participation in activities and organizations; fifteen to thirty items of educational and employment history and career experiences; and thirty or more spaces for additional locally designed questions and comments.

Some college and university Web sites contain copies of surveys and research results from their alumni studies. Often these are embedded in the institution's accreditation self-study document. Here are some good examples:

- Georgia Tech employs a well-designed alumni survey that assesses gains in knowledge and skill, satisfaction with many aspects of the undergraduate experience, and postgraduate education, professional development, and employment. The Office of Assessment generates useful reports from these surveys, and the report's appendix contains a copy of the survey instrument. http://www.assessment.gatech.edu/wp-content/uploads/GR_2006_Alum_Institute_RPT_FINAL_12_7_2007.pdf.
- Indiana University-Purdue University Indianapolis has surveyed recent graduates since the early 1990s and recently began to collect data from graduates five years out. http://www.imir.iupui.edu/infore/infore_recentalumni.asp.
- Massachusetts Institute of Technology has developed a number of good survey instruments, an alumni survey among them. http://web.mit.edu/ir/surveys/.
- New Jersey Institute of Technology periodically surveys its alumni and shares the results online. http://www.njit.edu/irp/reports/2005/Alumni_Survey_Fall_2005_safe_fonts.ppt#256,1,Alumni Survey Fall 2005.
- Penn State's Center for the Study of Higher Education developed an alumni survey as part of its national study of over two hundred engineering programs. http://www.ed.psu.edu/educ/ec2000/survey-instruments/alumni-survey.
- At Texas A&M University-Corpus Christi, the Office of Planning and Institutional Effectiveness administers an alumni survey every two years to assess the effectiveness of the university. www.youtube.com/watch?v=-mVpGmoES3w&NR=1.

Conclusion

Most institutions survey their graduates to collect information on employment and additional degrees earned, especially when preparing an accreditation self-study. Unfortunately such efforts rarely include comparative benchmarks or analysis of collegiate experiences that may have produced the reported results. The best alumni research examines outcomes that occur after college, not only to demonstrate institutional effectiveness (usually within the context of maintaining accreditation) but also to enhance alumni giving (usually within the context of meeting financial goals). Would alumni do it all over again? That is, would they attend the same institution? Select the same major? Enter the same career? And what campus experiences and precollege traits are most likely to influence their responses? ACT appears to offer one of the few commercially available instruments for asking alumni to evaluate their college education and its impact on their lives.

Such alumni feedback attracts attention on and off the campus. Colleges and universities have moved toward a more outcomes-based approach to assessment as a result of increasing pressures from employers, trustees, government, and accreditation bodies. Because they have legitimacy with these various stakeholders, alumni speak with a loud voice when they provide evidence of institutional effectiveness.

Alumni studies are useful not only to assess institutional effectiveness but also to aid institutional planning and revenue generation. Thus, institutional researchers who seek to maximize the utility of alumni research should develop partnerships that include administrative offices and academic departments alike. Alumni are important sources of information and support, and alumni studies should occupy a prominent place in the institutional research portfolio.

References

Astin, A. W. *Four Critical Years*. San Francisco: Jossey-Bass, 1977.

Astin, A. W. *What Matters in College*. San Francisco: Jossey-Bass, 1993.

Blau, P. M., and Duncan, O. D. *The American Occupational Structure*. New York: Wiley, 1967.

Borden, V. M. H. "Using Alumni Research to Align Program Improvement with Institutional Accountability." In D. Weerts and J. Vidal (eds.), *Enhancing Alumni Research: European and American Perspectives*. New Directions for Institutional Research, no. 126. San Francisco: Jossey-Bass, 2005.

Bowen, H. R. *Investment in Learning: The Individual and Social Value of American Higher Education*. San Francisco: Jossey-Bass, 1977.

Cabrera, A. F., Weerts, D. J., and Zulick, B. J. "Making an Impact with Alumni Surveys." In D. Weerts and J. Vidal (eds.), *Enhancing Alumni Research: European and American Perspectives*. New Directions for Institutional Research, no. 126. San Francisco: Jossey-Bass, 2005.

Delaney, A. M. "Ideas to Enhance Higher Education's Impact on Graduates' Lives: Alumni Recommendations." *Tertiary Education and Management*, 2004, *10*(2), 89–105.

Ewell, P. T. "Alumni Studies as Instruments of Public Policy: The U.S. Experience." In D. Weerts, and J. Vidal (eds.), *Enhancing Alumni Research: European and American Perspectives*. New Directions for Institutional Research, no. 126. San Francisco: Jossey-Bass, 2005.

Feldman, K. A., and Newcomb, T. M. *The Impact of College on Students*. San Francisco: Jossey-Bass, 1969.

Moden, G. O., and Williford, M. A. "Applying Alumni Research to Decision Making." In G. S. Melchiori (ed.), *Alumni Research: Methods and Applications*. New Directions in Institutional Research, no. 60. San Francisco: Jossey-Bass, 1988.

Murray, N. "The Graduates Survey, Step by Step." *Journal of Career Planning and Employment*, 1994, *54*(2), 36–39, 62–64.

Pace, C. R. *Measuring Outcomes of College: Fifty Years of Findings and Recommendations for the Future.* San Francisco: Jossey-Bass, 1979.

Pascarella, E. T., and Terenzini, P. T. *How College Affects Students.* (Vol. 2) San Francisco: Jossey-Bass, 2005.

Pettit, J., and Litten, L. H. (eds.). *A New Era of Alumni Research: Improving Institutional Performance and Better Serving Alumni.* New Directions for Institutional Research, no. 101. San Francisco: Jossey-Bass, 1999.

Schneider, S. C., and Niederjohn, R. J. "Assessing Student Learning Outcomes Using Graduating Senior Exit Surveys and Alumni Surveys." Frontiers in Education Conference Proceedings, Atlanta, GA, 1995. Retrieved February 9, 2010, from http://fie-conference.org/fie95/2c1/2c11/2c11.htm.

Sewell, W. H., and Hauser, R. M. *Education, Occupation, and Earnings.* Orlando, FL: Academic Press, 1975.

Shoemaker, D. (ed.). *Research in Alumni Relations.* Washington, DC: Council for Advancement and Support of Education, 1999.

Smart, J. C., and Pascarella, E. T. "Socioeconomic Achievements of Former College Students." *Journal of Higher Education*, 1986, *57*, 529–549.

Volkwein, J. F. "A Model of Alumni Gift-Giving Behavior." Paper presented at the Association for the Study of Higher Education, Atlanta, GA, Nov. 1989.

Volkwein, J. F. The Four Faces of Institutional Research. In J. F. Volkwein (ed.), *What Is Institutional Research All About: A Critical and Comprehensive Assessment of the Profession.* New Directions for Institutional Research, no. 104. San Francisco: Jossey-Bass, 1999.

Volkwein, J. F. "Assessing Institutional Effectiveness and Connecting the Pieces of a Fragmented University." In J. Burke (ed.), *Fixing the Fragmented University.* San Francisco: Jossey-Bass/Anker, 2007.

Volkwein, J. F., and Bian, F. "Undergraduate Experiences Associated with the Career Success and Satisfaction of Alumni." Paper presented at the NEAIR annual conference, Albany, NY, 1990.

Volkwein, J. F., and Bian, F. "Influences on Alumni Willingness to Attend the Same Institution, Select the Same Major, and Enter the Same Career." In D. Shoemaker (ed.), *Research in Alumni Relations.* Washington, DC: Case Books, 1999.

Volkwein, J. F., and Parmley, K. "Testing Why Alumni Give: A Model of Alumni Gift-Giving Behavior." In D. Shoemaker (ed.), *Research in Alumni Relations*, Washington, DC: Case Books, 1999.

Weerts, D., and Vidal, J. (eds.). *Enhancing Alumni Research: European and American Perspectives.* New Directions for Institutional Research, no. 126. San Francisco: Jossey-Bass, 2005.

Recommended Reading

Astin, A. W., Panos, R. J., and Creager, J. A. *National Norms for Entering College Freshmen—Fall 1966.* Washington, DC: American Council on Education, 1967.

Borden, V., and Zak Owens, J. *Measuring Quality: Choosing Among Surveys and Other College and University Quality Assessments.* Washington, DC: Association for Institutional Research and American Council on Education, 2001. Retrieved March 4, 2010, from http://www.airweb.org/images/measurequality.pdf.

Chickering, A. W. *Education and Identity.* San Francisco: Jossey-Bass, 1969.

Kuh, G. D. "Imagine Asking the Client: Using Student and Alumni Surveys for Account-ability in Higher Education." In J. Burke (ed.), *Achieving Accountability in Higher Education: Balancing Public, Academic, and Market Demands.* San Francisco: Jossey-Bass, 2005.

Melchiori, G. S. (ed.). *Alumni Research: Methods and Applications.* New Directions for Institutional Research, no. 60. San Francisco: Jossey-Bass, 1988.

Suskie, L. A. *Questionnaire Survey Research: What Works.* (2nd ed.) Tallahassee, FL: Association for Institutional Research, 1996.

J. FREDERICKS VOLKWEIN is emeritus professor of higher education at The Pennsylvania State University and a former director of the Center for the Study of Higher Education.

10

This chapter summarizes ten selected issues and common problems that arise in most assessment research projects and offers constructive suggestions for assessment researchers.

Measurement Issues in Assessment

J. Fredericks Volkwein, Alexander C. Yin

This chapter summarizes selected issues and problems that arise in most research projects. To a critical faculty audience, the data analysis and measurement problems that follow can be show-stoppers if they are not properly handled or defended:

- The uses of grades in assessment
- Institutional review boards
- Research design as a compromise
- Standardized testing
- Self-reported measures
- Missing data
- Weighting data
- Conditional effects
- Hierarchical linear modeling versus ordinary least squares
- Causation and correlation

The Use of Grades in Assessment

Perhaps the greatest obstacle to faculty support for assessment is the extra workload and the feeling that they already assess student performance in their courses. Most faculty members devote a great deal of effort to evaluating student learning in their courses and assigning grades, and they groan when they hear the word *assessment*. These course grades are aggregated each semester and over the student's career to produce a grade point average

NEW DIRECTIONS FOR INSTITUTIONAL RESEARCH, Assessment Supplement 2009, Spring 2010 © Wiley Periodicals, Inc.
Published online in Wiley InterScience (www.interscience.wiley.com) • DOI: 10.1002/ir.336

(GPA). The infamous GPA has grown to support a variety of uses, from academic probation to academic honors, from making remediation decisions to graduate school recommendations, from financial aid eligibility to employee hiring. However, grades in courses, as well as overall GPAs, have several limitations.

One limitation is the declining legitimacy of grades among stakeholders, especially employers. In the past two decades, the proportion of A grades at nearly all types of institutions, selective and unselective alike, has grown from about 30 percent to over 50 percent, and no one believes that the increase is justified by increases in student talent and effort. Quite the contrary, in fact.

A second serious limitation with grades is that faculty assign them using inconsistent standards. When they assign grades, some instructors use goal-driven or criterion-referenced evaluation: How well has the student met the learning goals in the course? Others use improvement-driven evaluation: How much has the student improved in knowledge or gained in skill? Still other professors use norm-referenced or comparison evaluation, and grade students on a normal curve, valuing each student's performance only in relation to others. In addition, some grade mostly on student effort: if students work hard and come to class regularly, they will probably get a good grade regardless of how much they have learned. Under these conditions, it is impossible to use cumulative grades as accurate reflections of student learning.

Faculty and department grading practices are both idiosyncratic and inconsistent, and this also contributes to the low predictive power of admissions credentials. The variability of grading standards from department to department, as well as from faculty member to faculty member, produces a generally low positive correlation between high school and college GPAs. Predicting college GPAs from SAT scores and high school records is also made difficult by the fact that the most talented students frequently enter the most demanding majors, like accounting, pre-med, pre-law, math, science, and engineering, where they may or may not receive high grades.

Moreover, student learning is multidimensional, so the grade in most cases is but a crude reflection of actual student performance. We currently have few means for faculty to indicate how the course, and the student's performance in it, contributes to the educated person. How does this course, and what the student learned in it, contribute to knowledge and skills required for success? The GPA in forty courses does not necessarily sum to an excellent undergraduate education.

The bottom line is that grades in courses would be appropriate for assessing student learning and outcomes if instructors were explicit about the standards they are using and assigned separate grades based on meeting objective standards or learning goals, on improvement or gains in knowledge, on student effort and punctuality, and on normative comparison or rank in class. In the absence of such clarity, grades must be supplemented by other evidence of student learning.

Institutional Review Boards

After questionable research involving human participants, the National Commission for the Protection of Human Subjects of Biomedical and Behavioral Research was created in 1974 to protect the welfare of human test subjects. The commission released the Belmont Report in 1979, which created three guiding principles of institutional review boards (IRBs):

- Full assessment of the risks and benefits of the research considered and justified by the researcher
- Fair selection of research participants
- Informed consent, which includes ensuring voluntary participation and presentation of adequate information about risks and benefits

The Code of Federal Regulations (CFR) lays out some guidelines on the operation of IRBs. A human participant is defined as "a living individual about whom an investigator (whether professional or student) conducting research obtains: 1) data through intervention or interaction with the individual or 2) identifiable private information" (45 CFR sec. 46.102[f]). The most perplexing issue for institutional researchers is determining whether their projects involving students and faculty are subject to IRB review. In general, if the project is for internal decision making and quality improvements at the university, the institutional researcher will not need IRB approval. If the research is for public distribution or publication, and certainly if the research is funded by an external sponsor, an IRB review is usually required.

Within the IRB, the CFR stipulates three levels of review: exempt, expedited, and full. Exempt reviews consist of research within an educational setting involving classroom educational practices, educational tests, internal administrative questionnaires, and the study of existing data that are publicly available. These reviews are exempt from federal oversight because the risk is low. However, this has not prevented some heavily regulatory states, or some universities, from requiring more review than required by federal law. Most projects conducted by institutional researchers using campus databases are exempt. Also exempt are analyses of on-the-shelf existing data to which a researcher has been granted access that does not include identifiable private information about individuals. Thus, research using national databases where the respondents cannot be identified, including survey data from sources like the National Center for Education Statistics, National Center for Higher Education Management Systems, Higher Education Research Institute, and National Survey of Student Engagement

(NSSE), is not "human participant" research as defined by the Department of Health and Human Services federal regulations.

Expedited reviews are projects that include the normal kinds of administrative data collected on students and employees along with new data collection activities where the subjects are clearly not at risk and likely to give permission to be interviewed or fill out a survey. Full review projects usually involve children, prisoners, pregnant women, the mentally ill, and other vulnerable populations, especially if medical, environmental, or even psychological interventions are proposed. In a full review, the IRB determines if the risks are balanced by sufficient benefits. In addition to federal law, institutional researchers must review their campus and state policies to ensure that their research is in compliance, especially if the research collects information from current students, faculty, and employees rather than analyzing historical data previously collected.

Most IRBs at least look at the following issues when reviewing protocols: how much risk exists for the research subjects and whether the potential benefits of the research outweigh those risks. Are the participants adequately informed about the research procedures before consenting to participate? Does the research protocol adequately protect private information? Is the recruitment of research participants equitable and nonthreatening? Institutional researchers may encounter issues related to merging new data from research participants with old administrative records. Respondent confidentiality and data security need to be maintained. Many IRBs require the destruction of confidential data at the conclusion of a study, thus hampering subsequent longitudinal studies unless they are designed and approved that way at the beginning.

Understanding and following the IRB protocols will improve the relationship between institutional researchers and the IRB office. Tension can occur because the institutional research mission is to uncover information to improve the organization, while the IRB mission is to protect participants from harmful information being revealed. Thus, institutional researchers need to be acquainted with the IRB policies at their institution and develop a comfortable working relationship by educating the IRB staff about the goals and mission of the institutional research function.

Research Design as a Compromise

In Chapter Three, Terenzini states that research design is a series of compromises. Scientifically controlled experiments are rare in the social sciences because it is difficult to control conditions and people. As I discussed in Chapter Two, each type of research question drives the researcher in a different direction for data collection and analysis, and as noted throughout this volume, each research design and assessment instrument has advantages and disadvantages. All research involves finding the right balance of methodological strengths and weaknesses—knowing what is being gained and what is being given away in each research design (Terenzini, 1989). Comparison measurement allows benchmarking student performance but tells little about student gains. A pretest/posttest allows documenting student gains but may not necessarily indicate that the student has attained the necessary level of knowledge or skill. Cross-sectional designs yield quicker results but must guard against sampling error and may yield no information about student growth. Longitudinal studies can be more powerful but may take several years for useful results, and they nearly always suffer from participant attrition. A locally designed ex post facto study may be relatively inexpensive to conduct, but causal statements are not possible.

Standardized Testing

Chapters Five through Eight review many of the standardized tests that are administered and scored uniformly to ensure that results can be compared across institutions and across time. Several of these chapters summarize the pros and cons of using a locally designed versus a commercial test, and we outlined the advantages and disadvantages of some of the most widely used standardized tests used for assessing basic skills, general education knowledge, personal growth, and attainment in the major.

What is the place of standardized tests in an assessment program? Suskie (2009) states that instruments have value if they match learning goals, measure what they purport to measure, and are part of a multiple measures approach to assessing student learning; if you give students compelling reasons to complete them and take them seriously; and if they provide useful information that will improve the student learning experience. In any case, standardized tests provide real advantages: their expert construction (usually in consultation with a national panel), their link to national norms, and the savings to the institution of instrument development and scoring. However, the institution and its faculty need to assure themselves that the standardized test is congruent with their curricular goals and that the norms are derived from appropriate and relevant comparison groups.

Selecting a standardized test has three important considerations: validity, reliability, and feasibility. Validity is accuracy—the ability of the instrument to assess accurately the domain or content of interest. Reliability is consistency—how much error a score contains. Feasibility is the ease of administration and costs (especially if commercial tests need to be purchased).

The following resources may help in selecting potential published instruments, and additional readings are listed in the references. *Mental Measurements Yearbook* and *Tests in Print* are both published by the Buros Institute and are available in many college libraries:

- *Mental Measurements Yearbook:* http://buros.unl.edu/buros/jsp/search.jsp
- *Tests in Print:* http://www.unl.edu/buros/bimm/html/howtotip.html
- *The NPEC Sourcebook on Assessment,* Volume 1: *Definitions and Assessment Methods for Critical Thinking, Problem Solving, and Writing:* http://nces .ed.gov/pubs2000/2000195.pdf

In fact, there is no standardized test (or, for that matter, any one test) that will ever be able to assess accurately four years of learning (or even one semester) in a couple of hours. Thus, it is wise to use multiple methods and measures for assessing student outcomes.

Self-Reported Measures

Developing relevant tests of student learning and skills can be difficult, time-consuming, and costly. Moreover, motivating students to perform their best on any test is a challenge. Hence, the use of self-reported outcomes is increasingly widespread, especially in research on college students and alumni. Since the 1970s, empirical studies have examined the adequacy of self-reported academic performance, learning outcomes, and skill develop- ment as proxies for actual or tested measures. This research indicates a mod- erate to strong correspondence between students' self-reports and more objective measures, especially when certain conditions are present.

In a meta-analysis of forty-four studies comparing self-reported versus actual grades and test scores, Kuncel, Crede, and Thomas (2005) found average correlations between self-reported and actual SAT scores of .82 and between self-reported and actual college GPAs of .90. Only the very lowest- performing students significantly misrepresent their grades and scores (the bottom 5 to 15 percent).

Substantial evidence supports the connection between self-reported learning and growth and objectively measured test performance. The social science literature indicates that student self-reports have only moderately positive correlations with objective measures when used to gauge the learn- ing or skill of individuals, but when aggregated to compare the performance of groups, the reliability of self-reported measures is quite high and is gen- erally considered to be a valid measure of real differences in learning between groups (Anaya, 1999; Pace, 1985; Pike, 1995, 1996). In their reviews of the literature, Pascarella and Terenzini (1991, 2005) conclude that the evidence from studies using self-reports of student learning is gen- erally consistent with evidence employing standardized tests. Although results vary depending on the traits and instruments examined, studies of individual test takers report correlations of .50 to .70 between self-reports and objective criterion measures on such instruments as the ACT Compre- hensive Test, the College Basic Academic Subjects Examination, and the Graduate Record Examination.

Thus, social science researchers generally believe that under the right conditions, student self-reports are both valid and reliable, especially for measuring and comparing the outcomes for groups of students rather than for comparing individuals. These desirable conditions are summarized by Hayek, Carini, O'Day, and Kuh (2002) and Kuh (2005) as follows: (1) the information requested is known to the respondents; (2) the questions are phrased clearly and unambiguously; (3) the questions refer to recent activities; (4) the respondents think the questions merit a serious and thoughtful response; and (5) answering the questions does not threaten, embarrass, or violate the privacy of the respondent or encourage the respondent to answer in socially desirable, rather than truthful, ways. Many assessment instruments meet these criteria (Borden and Zak Owens, 2001).

Many scholars have concluded that student self-reported growth and learning represent potentially useful and convenient alternatives to the more expensive and time-consuming standardized tests. However, some researchers have raised caution flags. Pascarella (2001) argues that students may come to college predisposed to report growth, or lack of it, and our assessment studies rarely measure students' precollege receptivity to educational experiences and their predisposition to report growth as the result of such experiences. "Unless this precollege disposition is controlled statistically," Pascarella notes, "it is quite likely that it will seriously confound the associations between various college experiences and student self-reported growth in college" (p. 491).

Another caution appears in a 2009 paper by Porter, who questions the validity of most college student surveys, especially those that collect information on student experiences and student outcomes simultaneously. Such student self-reports may be biased toward putting the student in a good light. Porter concludes that the vague wording of questions and response scales in many surveys contributes to misinterpretation and error. A 2010 study by Pascarella, Seifert, and Blaich addresses this problem and finds tentative support for the predictive utility of the NSSE Benchmarks. Using a pretest/posttest method at nineteen diverse institutions of higher education, the authors write, "Our findings suggest the dimensions of undergraduate experience measured by the NSSE benchmarks are, in fact, precursors to important educational outcomes."

These cautionary notes give additional support to the desirability of a multiple-indicator assessment strategy with a mix of direct and indirect measures of student learning (Pascarella and Terenzini, 2005).

Missing Data

Almost every survey contains incomplete answers and missing responses. Can you afford to throw out all the cases with missing data? What if most of the missing responses are accounted for by two or three survey items?

Are those bad items that should be discarded? What if most survey respondents have missing or blank responses on only a few items, but a small number have a high proportion of missing responses? At what point does the proportion of blank or missing responses on a survey call the validity of the entire case into question? Deleting cases can be dangerous, because the incomplete ones may be needed to produce a sample that is fully representative of the population. Even if the statistical procedure does not require complete data in every case (such as ordinary least squares regression), there may be good reasons to plug in missing information in a data file. Suppose you are building multi-item scales, and you need a value for each item in the scale?

Most researchers use decision rules to decide when to replace missing data versus throw out the entire case. Depending on the nature of the data and the number of "good cases," researchers tend to keep cases with less than 20 percent missing and throw out cases with more than 40 percent missing. Between 20 and 40 percent is debatable. Some information is better than none. Therefore, researchers have developed an array of techniques for salvaging cases by carefully replacing the missing data.

This section offers suggestions for handling missing data; however, preventive measures are always better than reactive actions. The best way to treat missing data is to prevent them from occurring. Careful research design and data collection can limit not only the amount of item nonresponse but also the amount of unit nonresponse (people who do not take the survey at all). Before sending out surveys, institutional researchers should carefully examine the survey questions and structure in order to maximize response rates. Using test groups to pilot-test the survey can prevent many problems and stresses later. It is always better to have actual data than to use techniques to deal with missing data.

The traditional strategies for handling missing data are variable deletion, listwise deletion, pairwise deletion, and single imputation. If a certain variable contains the majority of the missing values and the variable is inconsequential to the results, it may be wise to delete the variable from the dataset.

Listwise or *casewise deletion* is the removal of cases with any missing values. The drawbacks of removing cases are the possibility of diminishing representativeness and depleting the statistical power of a study by removing too many cases from the data set, making the analysis useless.

Pairwise deletion uses all the available data in the analysis, where the means, standard deviations, and a correlation matrix between variables are calculated. These values are used as inputs for an appropriate statistical procedure, such as ordinary least squares regression, to help estimate the missing value. Pairwise deletion, though, is ill advised when the missing values are not randomly distributed through the data set. Pairwise deletion must be carefully used because as the sample sizes vary across pairs of variables, the greater is the likelihood that a pairwise deletion will not produce a covariance structure.

Single imputation uses the available data to estimate a value for the missing data. Common single imputation includes replacing data with the mean response or the mode. Other alternatives are estimating values based on relationships with other variables (conditional mean approach). For example, instead of using the mean of the whole data set, use the mean of the cases that have characteristics similar to the case with the missing value.

With computer software becoming more powerful, institutional researchers can now employ statistical methodologies that use complex mathematical algorithms to replace missing data, such as imputation with expectation maximization (EM) and multiple imputation. The *EM method* approaches the missing data by answering, "What parameter estimates are most likely given data that were observed?" This algorithm is an iterative process that does not stop until the estimates of parameters from one cycle to the next are deemed inconsequential. Although the EM method is superior to traditional approaches, it does not consider estimations of unknown precision. Rather, estimations represent one possible solution in an uncertain range of possibilities.

Multiple imputations address this issue by estimating a number of possible values for the missing value. A Markov chain Monte Carlo estimation is used to generate the possible values. Institutional researchers can create a number of imputed data sets and then perform analyses of interest on each one. Parameter estimates can then be combined across each of these analyses to yield better estimates and a picture of the variability of these estimates among the various imputed data sets. As few as five imputed data sets have been shown to provide satisfactory results.

Weighting Data

Sometimes in the collection of data, researchers do not get alignment between respondents and the actual population. In weighting data, there are two simple rules. The first is to make sure you know the characteristic in question (for example, class year, sex, race) for all the people in the population and all the people in the sample, and the second is to be sure that the characteristic is correlated with the outcome. For example, if the characteristic (say, in state versus out of state) is not correlated with the outcome, then you probably do not need to weight for it.

Consider the problem faced by Julie Alig when she was an institutional researcher at Saint Anselm College in New Hampshire. She had outcomes survey data from multiple classes of graduating seniors and observed that responses by class year and sex were uneven across the years. She also knew that the self-reported outcomes and levels of satisfaction differed significantly between males and females, and probably by class year as well. Thus, the unevenness in responses may generate conclusions that do not accurately portray the general population of graduates or the trends. Alig needed to weight the data on sex and year of graduation so that the sample of respondents better reflected the population of graduating seniors, thus reducing sampling error.

To weight on two variables, first do so on the one that is more out of alignment with the actual population (say, male-female). Using either male or female as an anchor, multiply the other cases by X. For example, if the male-to-female split among survey respondents is 30 to 70 but the actual population is 50–50, adjust the data by multiplying either the male cases by 1.67 or the female cases by .714 to bring them into 50–50 alignment.

After weighting on sex, rerun the frequencies and see if the survey respondents are still out of alignment on graduation year (they may not be if male-to-female imbalance was the main cause of the problem). Then if the class year numbers are still out of balance, take the new (sex-adjusted) data file and apply graduation year weights by multiplying each graduation year times its weight, using the highest or lowest year as an anchor. This has the effect of multiplying each case by the two weights and should give a survey response group that closely resembles the actual population of seniors across the years. This becomes clear by checking the frequencies after applying the weights. (For additional information and references on weighting, see Thomas, Heck, and Bauer [2005].)

Best practice tip: Always compute the weights using a copied file so that you can go back to the original unweighted data in case you make a mistake. In theory, however, you can use the same file in SPSS with the weights either turned on or off, but you should always store a backup copy of primary data sets and key analyses in a safe location.

Conditional Effects

Another effect to consider when analyzing data are conditional effects, also referred to as interactions. For example, say that you are conducting a study on the attrition of first-year students. You have a living-learning program in one of the residence halls on campus, so you include a variable for this program. The data reveal that it does make a difference whether students participate in the program, but that difference depends on whether the student is male or female. For example, the living-learning program may have a significantly positive effect on females but make no difference for males. (For more information about the analysis of conditional effects, see Coughlin [2005], especially the chapter by Ploutz-Snyder.)

Hierarchical Linear Modeling Versus Ordinary Least Squares

Chapter Two discussed the Volkwein Effectiveness Model and identified the various levels of evaluation and quality assurance. A common methodological issue in any research project is deciding on the unit of analysis. Is it the individual student? A department or program? The institution? Where do you expect change to occur and to be measurable? Multilevel analysis offers perhaps the best way to understand the impact of larger structures on the subunits within them.

Hierarchical linear modeling (HLM) has recently become the weapon of choice for untangling the effects of multiple institutions and departments on students. For example, you might use a multilevel analysis to examine student athletes across all the institutions within an athletic conference or national sports division. Some of the variation in the outcome (like GPA or graduation rate) may be due to differences in the individual students, some due to the particular sport, and some due to the influence of each institution and its culture. The first level of analysis would be the individual student variables (you might be measuring academic performance, graduation rates, and entering academic credentials). The second level of the analysis would be institutions. You might look at each institution's admissions selectivity, enrollment size, financial revenue per student, and the mission or highest degree offered. The third level of analysis would be each sport (football, basketball, baseball, volleyball, swimming, gymnastics, and tennis). (In this example, one could argue that the levels for institution and sport might be reversed.) In any case, by including these multiple levels of measurement, you can examine the influence of each on the dependent measure.

However, several researchers (Ethington, 1997; Porter, 2005; Smart, 2005) urge caution when deciding to use multilevel analysis such as HLM over single-level analysis like ordinary least squares (OLS) regression. Sometimes we get infatuated with fancy statistics that do not really add to understanding, and OLS output certainly is easier to interpret and explain than HLM. The common rule of thumb suggests the use of multilevel modeling only when the variation in the dependent variable between groups (in this case, students, sports, and institutions) exceeds 5 percent. "One should not be surprised if multilevel modeling results are very similar to OLS results when the ICC is less than 5%" (Porter, 2005, p. 120). There is no need to use a snow blower for a one-inch snowfall on a short walkway when a shovel suffices.

Correlation and Causation

When reporting their results, researchers need to guard against the confusion between correlation and causation. A relationship between two highly correlated variables may not necessarily be causal. For example, a study of youth between the ages of two and twenty will probably show a high correlation between IQ and foot size. Although the greater the foot size, the more intelligent a person, the relationship between the two variables is not causal. Foot size and IQ no doubt result from a third "cause": as children grow older and larger, they develop both physically (foot size) and cognitively (IQ).

Chapter Four discussed the value of using an assessment model because it provides a theoretical and rational basis for expecting to find a statistical relationship or correlation between certain predictor variables and particular outcomes. When the expected association between two variables is verified empirically, there is a logical basis for believing in their causal relationship. Using a causal model (such as the Terenzini-Reason Comprehensive Model) is useful because it provides information on how to improve student outcomes by changing the student experiences and programs that produce those outcomes. For example, a study may show that students who received supplemental instruction have better grades than those who did not receive this instruction. Using an outcomes model is likely to identify the variables that need to be controlled in order for an analysis to demonstrate a causal link between the supplemental instruction and better grades.

Since multiple student, environmental, and institutional characteristics can influence student learning and outcomes, most researchers find that they need healthy doses of multivariate inferential statistical procedures that use one or more independent variables (also known as indicator or predictor variables) to explain the dependent (outcome) variable.

Most assessment researchers find that parsimonious models are superior to complex models for communicating effectively to campus audiences. Thus, factor analysis, scale building, and other forms of data reduction are wise investments at the beginning of analysis. Exploratory factor analysis is used to explore the interrelationships among variables to discern whether they can be grouped into a smaller set of underlying factors. Confirmatory factor analysis is used to confirm the existence of a preexisting factor structure, like the concepts in an outcomes model. Whether testing a model or using one to guide the analysis, path analysis and structural equation modeling are highly desirable. In path analysis, multiple predictor variables are used in a linear model to predict or explain one or more criterion measures. Path analysis features the predictive ordering of variables, thus allowing the researcher to test an integrated theory of influences among a set of variables (Coughlin, 2005).

Conclusion

This chapter does not provide an in-depth review of everything institutional researchers need to know about measurement issues, but it gives a general sense of important concerns and pitfalls. In addition, there are constraints about doing assessment in an applied setting and often you have to settle for the best you can get. Although an assessment study might not be perfect, it needs to be sound enough to support policy and decision making aimed at constructive change, and the results need to be communicated effectively, the topic of the final chapter.

References

Anaya, G. "College Impact on Student Learning: Comparing the Use of Self-Reported Gains, Standardized Test Scores, and College Grades." *Research in Higher Education*, 1999, *40*, 499–526.

Belmont Report. 1979. Retrieved February 9, 2010, from http://www.hhs.gov/ohrp/humansubjects/guidance/belmont.htm.

Borden, V., and Zak Owens, J. *Measuring Quality: Choosing Among Surveys and Other College and University Quality Assessments.* Washington, DC: Association for Institutional Research and American Council on Education, 2001. Retrieved March 4, 2010, from http://www.airweb.org/images/measurequality.pdf.

Coughlin, M. A. "Applied Multivariate Statistics." In M. A. Coughlin (ed.), *Applications of Intermediate/Advanced Statistics in Institutional Research.* Tallahassee, FL: Association for Institutional Research, 2005.

Ethington, C. "A Hierarchical Linear Modeling Approach to Studying College Effects." In J. C. Smart (ed.), *Higher Education: Handbook of Theory and Research.* (Vol. 12) New York: Agathon, 1997.

Hayek, J. C., Carini, R. M., O'Day, P. T., and Kuh, G. D. "Triumph or Tragedy: Comparing Student Engagement Levels of Members of Greek-Letter Organizations and Other Students." *Journal of College Student Development*, 2002, 43(5), 643–663.

Kuh, G. D. "Using Student and Alumni Surveys for Accountability in Higher Education." In J. C. Burke (ed.), *The Many Faces of Accountability.* San Francisco: Jossey-Bass, 2005.

Kuncel, N. R., Crede, M., and Thomas, L. L. "The Validity of Self-Reported Grade Point Averages, Class Ranks, and Test Scores: A Meta-Analysis and Review of the Literature." *Review of Educational Research*, 2005, 75, 63–82.

Pace, C. R. *The Credibility of Student Self-Reports.* Los Angeles: University of California, Center for the Study of Evaluation, Graduate School of Education, 1985.

Pascarella, E. "Using Student Self-Reported Gains to Estimate College Impact: A Cautionary Tale." *Journal of College Student Development*, 2001, 42, 488–492.

Pascarella, E. T., Seifert, T. A., and Blaich, C. (2010). "How Effective Are the NSSE Benchmarks in Predicting Important Educational Outcomes?" *Change*, Jan./Feb. 2010. Retrieved February 5, 2010, from http://www.changemag.org/Archives/Back%20Issues/January-February%202010/full-how-effective.html.

Pascarella, E. T., and Terenzini, P. T. "Appendix: Methodological and Analytical Issues in Assessing the Influence of College." In E. T. Pascarella and P. T. Terenzini (eds.), *How College Affects Students: Findings and Insights from Twenty Years of Research.* San Francisco: Jossey-Bass, 1991.

Pascarella, E. T., and Terenzini, P. T. *How College Affects Students: A Third Decade of Research.* San Francisco: Jossey Bass, 2005.

Pike, G. R. "The Relationships Between Self-Reports of College Experiences and Achievement Test Scores." *Research in Higher Education*, 1995, 36, 1–22.

Pike, G. R. "Limitations of Using Students' Self-Reports of Academic Development as Proxies for Traditional Achievement Measures." *Research in Higher Education*, 1996, 37, 89–114.

Porter, S. R. "What Can Multilevel Models Add to Institutional Research?" In M. A. Coughlin (ed.), *Applications of Intermediate/Advanced Statistics in Institutional Research.* Tallahassee, FL: Association for Institutional Research, 2005.

Porter, S. R. "Do College Student Surveys Have Any Validity?" Paper delivered at the Association for the Study of Higher Education Annual Meeting. Vancouver, B.C., 2009.

Smart, J. C. "Attributes of Exemplary Research Manuscripts Employing Quantitative Analysis." *Research in Higher Education*, 2005, 46(4), 461–477.

Suskie, L. (2009). "Selecting a Published Test or Survey." In L. Suskie, *Assessing Student Learning: A Common Sense Guide.* (2nd ed.) San Francisco: Jossey-Bass/Wiley, 2009.

Terenzini, P. T. "Assessment with Open Eyes: Pitfalls in Studying Student Outcomes." *Journal of Higher Education*, 1989, 60, 644–664.

Thomas, S. L., Heck, R. H., and Bauer, K. W. "Weighting and Adjusting for Design Effects in Secondary Data Analyses." In P. Umbach (ed.), *Survey Research: Emerging Issues*, New Directions for Institutional Research, no. 127. San Francisco: Jossey-Bass, 2005.

Recommended Reading

Allison, P. *Missing Data*. Thousand Oaks: Sage, 2002.

American Educational Research Association. *Standards for Educational and Psychological Testing* (2nd ed.) Washington, DC: Author, 2000.

Baird, L. L. *Using Self-Reports to Predict Student Performance*. New York: College Board, 1976.

Banta, T., and Associates (eds.), *Building a Scholarship of Assessment*. San Francisco: Jossey-Bass, 2002.

Coughlin, M. A. *Applications of Intermediate Advanced Statistics in Institutional Research*. Tallahassee, FL: Association for Institutional Research, 2005.

Croninger, R. G., and Douglas, K. M. "Missing Data and Institutional Researchers." In P. Umbach (ed.), *Survey Research: Emerging Issues*, New Directions for Institutional Research, no. 127. San Francisco: Jossey-Bass, 2005.

Gonyea, R. M. "Self-Reported Data in Institutional Research: Review and Recommendations." In P. Umbach (ed.), *Survey Research: Emerging Issues*. New Directions for Institutional Research, no. 127. San Francisco: Jossey-Bass, 2005.

Hopkins, K. D. *Educational and Psychological Measurement and Evaluation*. Needham Heights, MA: Allyn & Bacon, 1997.

Kennedy, J. M. "Institutional Review Boards and Institutional Researchers." In P. Umbach (ed.), *Survey Research: Emerging Issues*. New Directions for Institutional Research, no. 127. San Francisco: Jossey-Bass, 2005.

Krathwohl, D. R. *Methods of Educational and Social Science Research: The Logic of Methods*. (3rd ed.) Long Grove, IL: Waveland Press, 2009.

Pascarella, E. T., Cruce, T., Umbach, P. D., Wolniak, G. C., Kuh, G. D., Carini, R. M. et al. "Institutional Selectivity and Good Practices in Undergraduate Education: How Strong Is the Link?" *Journal of Higher Education*, 2006, 77(2), 251–285.

Pike, G. R. "Measurement Issues in Outcomes Assessment." In T. Banta and Associates (eds.), *Building a Scholarship of Assessment*. San Francisco: Jossey-Bass, 2002.

Ploutz-Snyder, R. J. "Analysis of Variance Applications in Institutional Research?" In M. A. Coughlin (ed.), *Applications of Intermediate/Advanced Statistics in Institutional Research*. Tallahassee, FL: Association for Institutional Research, 2005.

Terenzini, P. T., Cabrera, A. F., Colbeck, C. L., Parente, J. M., and Bjorklund, S. A. "Collaborative Learning vs. Lecture/Discussion: Students' Reported Learning Gains." *Journal of Engineering Education*, 2001, 90, 123–130.

J. FREDERICKS VOLKWEIN is emeritus professor of higher education at The Pennsylvania State University and a former director of the Center for the Study of Higher Education.

ALEXANDER C. YIN is a senior project associate of the Center for the Study of Higher Education at The Pennsylvania State University.

11

Assessment research is at its best when it packages research results and data so that they can be digested by multiple audiences.

Reporting Research Results Effectively

J. Fredericks Volkwein

After reading the previous chapters of this volume, you should be feeling comfortable about the kinds of issues you need to consider before undertaking an assessment study. You know that you need to ask why and to clarify the inspirational and pragmatic purposes of the assessment. To what extent is the study aimed at educational improvement internally and to what extent aimed at external accountability? Are the results expected to demonstrate goal attainment, improvement, comparison to others, meeting standards, cost-effective investment? These questions will drive the research design.

You know that you need to address the who question and target those from whom assessment data are being collected. Are you measuring the knowledge and skills of individuals and making decisions about their remediation, certification, or development? Or are you sampling from important populations of students and comparing them with each other, with themselves over a period of time, or perhaps with national norms?

We have also given you some ideas about what the objects of assessment are: basic skills, general education knowledge, attainment in the major, personal growth, attitudes and satisfaction, and alumni outcomes—cognitive and noncognitive alike. Finally this volume has set out some conceptual models, research methods, and data collection strategies and instruments so that you know how to carry out an assessment project. This chapter concludes the volume by underscoring the importance of communicating the findings effectively.

NEW DIRECTIONS FOR INSTITUTIONAL RESEARCH, Assessment Supplement 2009, Spring 2010 © Wiley Periodicals, Inc.
Published online in Wiley InterScience (www.interscience.wiley.com) • DOI: 10.1002/ir.337

The importance of effective reporting is underscored by the Association for Institutional Research (AIR), which has published two volumes on the topic (Bers and Seybert, 1999; Sanders and Filkins, 2009) and has given Best Visual Presentation Awards at the AIR Annual Forum. After research design, data collection, and analysis, institutional researchers need to report their findings in an effective manner; otherwise their efforts will have been wasted. This chapter reviews some best practices for reporting research results to diverse audiences in written, visual, and verbal presentations.

Preparing Reports for Effective Communication

The two AIR volumes on this topic emphasize the need to shape research reports for diverse audiences: executive management, trustees, faculty, alumni, students, and parents, among others. A common expression in institutional research circles is that research results can be accurate, timely, and audience friendly but not all three. In the haste of preparation, reports can suffer from inadequate analysis, visual complexity, or unclear message. The impact of the findings may be diminished if a report overfocuses on the data and ignores the report's appearance and the audiences to which it is directed. Here are some guidelines from the AIR publications.

Consider the Audience. Recognize from the beginning that different audiences read reports for different reasons. By talking to members of the intended audiences or gathering feedback on what members of the audiences might like to know, you can better compile a report to meet the respective needs. In this step, you work backward from the end result that you would like to know and build a report that will allow readers to easily find the answers to their questions. The vice presidents for academic affairs, student affairs, and business affairs are likely to be interested in very different aspects of a student outcomes study. Although the overall format of the report will most likely vary with the topic being presented, the working-backward approach should be useful regardless of the report's final format.

You may need smaller versions of a larger, comprehensive report about a particular project. These small versions can be tailored to the respective needs of the various readers. For example, one could be to inform, while another may be to persuade. The faculty senate, the student affairs staff, and the development office are likely to be interested in very different findings from an alumni study. The smaller reports may contain varying degrees and complexities of reported information and can take different formats: written, oral, or electronic. As Bers and Seybert (1999) point out, "Clearly, a single report is rarely suitable for multiple uses, but institutional researchers rarely consider or take the time to prepare different versions of the same research project" (p. 31).

Regardless of the report's format, data and information must be presented so that they are "consumable for and thus useful to" each audience (Bers and Seybert, 1999, p. 5). A common practice places important results, briefly stated, in the body of the report, while details of statistical procedures and complete data tables are moved to appendixes or placed in longer, stand-alone documents. The main report can refer to the complete procedures and results that are available elsewhere. This practice not only allows for easier digestion of the report's contents by a greater number of people, but it also gives interested individuals access to the detailed research procedures and findings.

Providing the detailed information in appendixes or in a stand-alone report also follows an excellent practice outlined in section II(g) of the AIR Code of Ethics: "The institutional researcher shall document the sources of information and the process of analysis in each task in sufficient detail to enable a technically qualified colleague to understand what was done and to verify that the work meets all appropriate standards and expectations."

Another recommended practice presents the key findings in both text and numerical or graphic formats. Dual presentation emphasizes the importance of the information and increases the likelihood that readers will remember it. However, including information in both forms (numerical and written text) must strike the right balance between emphasis and redundancy to avoid annoying readers.

Finally, most institutional research audiences appreciate the KISS principle (Keep It Simple and Short). Experienced researchers recommend that reports be kept simple and that they look professional. If multiple versions of the same report are not created, then a Contents page clearly listing where information may be found should be included. This will allow readers from any audience to more easily locate specific information contained in longer, more comprehensive reports. At the very least, an executive summary should be included at the front of longer reports so that busy readers can quickly understand the main thrust of a report without having to read the entire document.

Best practice tip: The use of simple descriptive statistics, such as counts, percentages, ratios, and averages, usually conveys a more powerful and understandable message than multivariate beta weights, factor loadings, eigenvalues, covariances, parameter estimates, and the like. When a multivariate analysis is crucial to the assessment results, experienced researchers strongly recommend the display of effect sizes to communicate the findings to campus audiences.

Preparing the Report. Assessment researchers should convey the information that multiple audiences need in a format (or variety of formats) that will allow readers to quickly find the information that they desire. Only in meeting the needs of the readers will institutional researchers have any hope in meeting their objectives of informing and persuading, or both. Here are some specific considerations for each part of the typical report.

Executive Summary. The executive summary may be the most important part of a report because it will be perhaps the most widely read, especially since most administrators, faculty, and trustees are busy people. This section usually contains a problem statement, perhaps a brief overview describing the research approach, and major findings and conclusions. Similar to a movie trailer, the executive summary needs to provide enough information for readers to understand the main purpose and findings of the study without getting into the details.

Introduction and Literature Review. The introduction orients the audience to the purpose of the assessment. In writing the introduction, understand who the readers are and why they may be reading the report. This is why, at the beginning of the assessment project, it helps to identify its purposes, goals, and audience. The introduction sets the tone for the rest of the report; thus, the report should open with something intriguing to attract the reader's interest.

Best practice tip: An extensive literature review is not usually necessary in writing these reports, but faculty audiences react positively to research that is conceptually grounded and recognizes the most important scholarship in the field. Pascarella and Terenzini's (2005) *How College Affects Students: A Third Decade of Research* is an invaluable resource tool that can provide information on the topic being assessed and what other similar studies have found. At the very least, the report should provide a context for the report's results by noting previous studies at the institution—for example, "Between 2000 and 2005, the institutional research office tracked first-year student retention and found that 70 percent persisted to their second year. The school implemented Seminars for First-Year Students in 2006, and the campus now wants to see if retention rates improved subsequently." Providing such a context assists readers in understanding the purpose and importance of the assessment.

Research Methods. This section summarizes the research design, or at least describes the research population examined, the variables measured, and the procedures for collecting and analyzing the data. Audience consideration is important here because it may not be necessary to go into detail about the statistical methodology used. Placing key technical information in an appendix is sufficient for most campus audiences.

Results and Findings. Depending on the purpose of the assessment and the audience, assessment results should highlight both positive and negative findings, telling a coherent and interesting story. In the findings, a picture is worth a thousand words. The most important findings should be presented in both text and visual formats but strike a balance between too many and too few graphics and color. Tables and graphs can help readers understand the key findings more effectively than presenting data only in the text of the report, but the use of three-dimensional graphics or too many colors may detract from the message. On the other hand, too few graphics and the absence of color may lead a reader to judge a report as boring or unprofessional.

Avoid misleading the audience by manipulating the way you report numbers. As an extreme example, let's say that program A increases the number of graduating seniors from one to two per year, improving its degree production by 100 percent. Program B also increases its degree production by the same number, from 100 to 101, or 1 percent. Reporting only the percentage increases gives a dramatically different picture than the frequencies do. Thus, institutional researchers should avoid a "plug-and-chug" mindset. Good institutional research requires an understanding of both measurement issues and principles of effective reporting.

Conclusions and Implications. The final section of the report offers informed commentary, which may include explaining the results and exploring needed actions. Here the writer emphasizes the important findings and their implications for academic policy and administrative practice. Depending on the assessment audience, the report may recommend action steps or additional research. This section also summarizes the limitations of the study and offers cautionary notes about the numbers. Both positive and negative findings may not be conclusive and may instead be symptomatic of a condition needing further research.

Assessment is not about good news exclusively but also about uncovering weaknesses so that improvement can take place. However, negative findings should be used constructively rather than punitively against faculty or staff. Suskie (2009) gives useful tips for communicating disappointing assessment results.

Writing Skills. Writing clearly and concisely is critical for all researchers when communicating their findings. Bers and Seybert (1999) emphasize its importance by devoting the first chapter of their volume to writing skills. In that chapter, they discuss Robert Lucas's four myths about writing:

Myth 1: Writing must be perfect the first time. *Fact:* Writing is a process that moves through a progressive series of stages, from rough draft to finished product. Push your yearnings for perfection to the end of the process.

Myth 2: Writing must be inspired and spontaneous. *Fact:* Like the first myth, writing is the product of a process. This process includes talking with others, collecting ideas, outlining thoughts, keeping track of notes, and sharing drafts.

Myth 3: Writing proceeds quickly. *Fact:* The writing process takes time.

Myth 4: Writing is inherently difficult. *Fact:* Good writing is a skill that can be developed with practice. More practice produces better writing.

Lucas (1996) gives six suggestions for writing more effectively:

- *Write regularly.* Lucas suggests setting aside time at least four days a week to practice writing. The time between sessions should be less than forty-eight hours.
- *Write in small amounts.* Each writing session should be about thirty minutes long. Lucas suggests writing in shorter, more frequent amounts.

NEW DIRECTIONS FOR INSTITUTIONAL RESEARCH • DOI: 10.1002/ir

- *Set a schedule.* Limit interruptions such as receiving visitors or phone calls.
- *Do not let writer's block inhibit writing sessions.* Each writing session does not have to be formal. Rather, it can be a time to brainstorm ideas or jot down notes.
- *Share writing early and often before it goes public.* The idea here is to solicit feedback from others because different perspectives and critiques are invaluable for improving one's writing.
- *Consult references about writing.* Engaging a writing mentor might be helpful.

The only one of these I disagree with is trying to write in thirty-minute bursts. Despite what Lucas says, I believe in writing momentum. If I have momentum, I never quit at the thirty-minute mark. But if you have writer's block, it helps to write something, *anything,* for half an hour.

Best practice tip: There are several style principles for clear writing, but the most important is the use of present tense and active voice to describe the research and its results. Using past tense and passive voice add wordiness and rarely engage the reader—for example, "This chapter was written to describe the characteristics of effective reporting, and we would like to thank you for reading it" versus "This chapter describes the characteristics of effective reporting, and we thank you for reading it."

Verbal Presentations

Almost every alumni study identifies public speaking as an important career skill, and assessment researchers need to be effective presenters in front of campus groups as well. If you are a speaker addressing an audience, the common wisdom suggests that you should tell them what you are going to say, say it, and then summarize what you said.

Verbal presentations and written reports enjoy many features in common. Both need to provide succinct information, coherently organized with major points connected in a logical sequence, clear representation of data, solid analysis, and a perceptive awareness of the different audiences. Both depend on the competence and preparatory efforts of the author. In both written and verbal formats, some effort is required to produce digestible information for the audience. And in both cases, mistakes are hard to correct. Written reports are often viewed as finished products and rarely revised after submission, whereas verbal reports are considered to be semi-finished, and the live presentation allows visual cues and audience feedback that can lead to an improved subsequent written report. However, those who have presented assessment results in person to campus management groups and conference sessions know that gaffes are difficult to live down.

There are basic presentation fundamentals unique to live audiences. Bers and Seybert (1999) and Sanders and Filkins (2009) provide helpful tips. Beebe and Beebe's (2006) book on public speaking is also useful. First, there are no retakes, so careful preparation of a script and even rehearsal in front of a mirror constitute wise practices. Eye contact, body language, verbal pace, delivery voice, and articulation all need attention. Think about what singers do to prepare for a solo performance, and deliver the message energetically. During your remarks, look at the audience and not at the screen, and never apologize for being nervous because you will just call attention to it and detract from your message.

Regarding the location of the presentation, remember that Murphy's law is at work, so arrive early to check out the facility and the equipment, and be prepared with paper backup. During the presentation, identify the major takeaways, not only at the end, but even earlier if you are presenting to the executive team. Be sure to leave time for questions, and respond constructively to hostile questions. During the question-and-answer period, be a good listener as well as respondent, so that you directly address the point of the inquiry. The key to successful presentations is to walk into the room knowing that you are the expert on the topic and that your prepared remarks and supporting visuals deliver a clear message.

Visual Display of Findings

Effective reporting requires the thoughtful integration of text and graphics. Under the leadership of Trudy Bers, AIR initiated the Best Visual Presentation Award to acknowledge that effective visual presentations are important communication tools in this work. Nearly all of us believe that data are more believable in a PowerPoint chart, and audiences have come to expect at least a few visuals in any report or presentation.

Although there are many different types of charts and tables, each aims to convey information as clearly as possible, whether to embellish a written document or a verbal presentation. In some cases, incorporating the charts within the document contributes to understanding; in others, the wiser decision is to add them as an appendix to avoid interrupting the flow of the text.

Bers and Seybert (1999) devote four chapters to discussing design principles for displaying data in tables and charts, and Sanders and Filkins (2009) summarize these in two chapters. In addition, Suskie (2009) offers some helpful tips for displaying data in reports and presentations. The helpful tips from these authors build directly from research on the ways that the eye and the mind absorb data and information (Kosslyn, 2006, 2007; Tufte, 2001, 2006). When constructing visuals in reports and presentations, here are some of the most important best practice tips from these various sources:

- Give each table and graph a meaningful, self-explanatory title so it can stand alone with minimal explanation, but avoid giving disproportionate space to titles, logos, or distracting backgrounds.

- Present variables according to some logic or organizing principle, such as size, date, or location.
- Use the KISS principle, and avoid putting too much information into one table or graph.
- Present the results so that they draw attention to the point you want the table or graph to make, and array the data in an order that makes sense to the audience and helps convey your point
- Make it easy for your audience to see differences and trends. Bars are usually better for displaying differences. Lines are usually better for displaying trends.
- Label lines and bars clearly, but try to avoid clutter like grid marks, tick marks, and slide background designs.
- Visuals are greatly enhanced by the effective use of color and pattern. Colors in adjacent bars or pies should have different levels of brightness. Avoid using colors of similar shade in adjacent regions, since the chart is likely to be photocopied in black and white at some point.
- Round decimals and fractions to whole numbers unless the exact numbers are important to the findings. Rarely do results need to display more than one decimal on a scale.
- Don't assume that a software-generated table or graph is easily readable.
- Use the appropriate type size and style for the audience. Most audiences require 24-point type or larger. Unreadable visuals are a quick way to lose audience attention.
- Rather than presenting a dense page of numbers showing the frequency distributions and means, use a bar chart to show the proportion scoring above and below the scale midpoint on each item.
- Avoid using three dimensions if only two dimensions are being portrayed.
- Place the dominant element of a bar or column at the bottom or left rather than in the middle.
- Join segments of adjacent bars or columns with lines to emphasize trends with column charts.
- Use a maximum of six segments in a pie chart. or six lines of data on a line graph. Using two or three is better.
- Date each graph and table, and note its source. Almost every table or chart can be improved, and multiple revisions create confusion if they are not dated.

Conclusion

Too many assessment researchers spend all their efforts planning and executing the research project with little attention to closing the loop at the end. If assessment findings are not communicated effectively, the process becomes an expensive exercise in research design and data collection. Appropriately packaging research results for diverse audiences becomes a priority once the data are collected and analysis begins. Written reports and

New Directions for Institutional Research • DOI: 10.1002/ir

verbal presentations need to be shaped with the audience in mind. Knowing what the audience wants or needs may be as important as knowing research methods and statistics. This chapter offers helpful tips and best practices for preparing written reports, verbal presentations, and supporting visuals. Thus equipped, researchers can give the assessment process the momentum it deserves.

References

Association for Institutional Research. Code of Ethics. Adopted by AIR membership 1992, Updates Approved by the AIR Board 2001. Tallahassee, FL. Retrieved February 10, 2010, from http://www.airweb.org/?page=140.

Beebe, S. A., and Beebe, S. J. *Public Speaking: An Audience Centered Approach* (6th ed.) Boston: Pearson Education, 2006.

Bers, T. H., and Seybert, J. A. *Effective Reporting*. Tallahassee, FL: Association for Institutional Research, 1999.

Kosslyn, S. *Graph Design for the Eye and Mind*. New York: Oxford University Press, 2006.

Kosslyn, S. *Clear and to the Point: Eight Psychological Principles for Compelling Power-Point Presentations*. New York: Oxford University Press, 2007.

Lucas, R. Keynote address. Association for Institutional Research Annual Forum Albuquerque, NM, 1996.

Pascarella, E., and Terenzini, P. T. *How College Affects Students: A Third Decade of Research* (Vol. 2). San Francisco: Jossey-Bass, 2005.

Sanders, L., and Filkins, J. *Effective Reporting* (2nd ed.). Tallahassee, FL: Association for Institutional Research, 2009.

Suskie, L. *Assessing Student Learning: A Common Sense Guide* (2nd ed.). San Francisco: Jossey-Bass, 2009.

Tufte, E. *The Visual Display of Quantitative Information* (2nd ed.). Cheshire, CT. Graphics Press, 2001.

Tufte, E. *The Cognitive Style of PowerPoint: Pitching Out Corrupts Within* (2nd ed.). Cheshire, CT: Graphics Press, 2006.

Recommended Reading

Smart, J. C. "Attributes of Exemplary Research Manuscripts Employing Quantitative Analysis." *Research in Higher Education*, 2005, 46(4), 461–477.

Walvoord, B. E. *Assessment Clear and Simple: A Practical Guide for Institutions, Departments and General Education*. San Francisco: Jossey-Bass, 2004.

J. FREDERICKS VOLKWEIN *is emeritus professor of higher education at The Pennsylvania State University and a former director of the Center for the Study of Higher Education.*

NEW DIRECTIONS FOR INSTITUTIONAL RESEARCH • DOI: 10.1002/ir

INDEX

NEW DIRECTIONS FOR INSTITUTIONAL RESEARCH

ORDER FORM SUBSCRIPTION AND SINGLE ISSUES

DISCOUNTED BACK ISSUES:

Use this form to receive 20% off all back issues of *New Directions for Institutional Research*.
All single issues priced at **$23.20** (normally $29.00)

TITLE	ISSUE NO.	ISBN
_____	_____	_____
_____	_____	_____
_____	_____	_____

Call 888-378-2537 or see mailing instructions below. When calling, mention the promotional code JBXND to receive your discount. For a complete list of issues, please visit www.josseybass.com/go/ndir

SUBSCRIPTIONS: (1 YEAR, 4 ISSUES)

☐ New Order   ☐ Renewal

U.S.	☐ Individual: $109	☐ Institutional: $264
CANADA/MEXICO	☐ Individual: $109	☐ Institutional: $304
ALL OTHERS	☐ Individual: $133	☐ Institutional: $338

Call 888-378-2537 or see mailing and pricing instructions below.
Online subscriptions are available at www.interscience.wiley.com

ORDER TOTALS:

Issue / Subscription Amount: $ _____

Shipping Amount: $ _____
(for single issues only – subscription prices include shipping)

Total Amount: $ _____

SHIPPING CHARGES:		
SURFACE	DOMESTIC	CANADIAN
First Item	$5.00	$6.00
Each Add'l Item	$3.00	$1.50

(No sales tax for U.S. subscriptions. Canadian residents, add GST for subscription orders. Individual rate subscriptions must be paid by personal check or credit card. Individual rate subscriptions may not be resold as library copies.)

BILLING & SHIPPING INFORMATION:

☐ **PAYMENT ENCLOSED:** *(U.S. check or money order only. All payments must be in U.S. dollars.)*

☐ **CREDIT CARD:**   ☐ VISA   ☐ MC   ☐ AMEX

Card number _____ Exp. Date _____

Card Holder Name _____ Card Issue # *(required)* _____

Signature _____ Day Phone _____

☐ **BILL ME:** *(U.S. institutional orders only. Purchase order required.)*

Purchase order # _____
Federal Tax ID 13559302 • GST 89102-8052

Name _____

Address _____

Phone _____ E-mail _____

Copy or detach page and send to: **John Wiley & Sons, PTSC, 5th Floor**
989 Market Street, San Francisco, CA 94103-1741

Order Form can also be faxed to: **888-481-2665**

PROMO JBXND

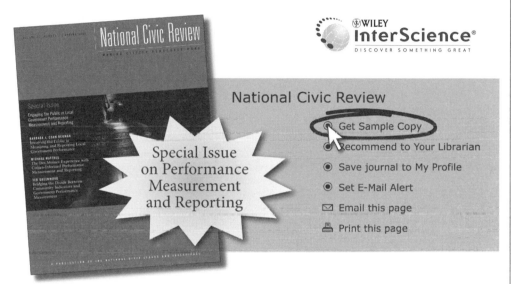